Easy to Use

PICK UP & PLAY

CLASSIC RIFFS

Licks & Riffs in the Style of Great Guitar Heroes

SEE IT ▦ HEAR IT

ALAN BROWN   JAKE JACKSON

Flame Tree Music

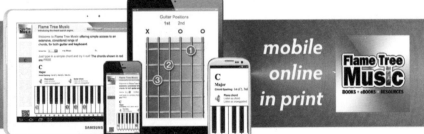

mobile
online
in print

Flame Tree Music
BOOKS • eBOOKS • RESOURCES

Contents

Publisher/Creative Director: Nick Wells • Layout Design: Jane Ashley • Website and Software: David Neville with Stevens Dumpala and Steve Moulton • Editorial: Gillian Whitaker

First published 2017 by
FLAME TREE PUBLISHING
6 Melbray Mews, Fulham,
London SW6 3NS, United Kingdom
flametreepublishing.com

Music information site: flametreemusic.com

17 18 19 20 21 22 23 • 1 2 3 4 5 6 7 8 9 10

The CIP record for this book is available from the British Library.

ISBN: 978-1-78664-239-4

All images and notation courtesy of Flame Tree Publishing Ltd, except the following: guitar diagrams © 2016 Jake Jackson/Flame Tree Publishing Ltd. Courtesy of Shutterstock.com and copyright the following photographers: Denis Belyaevskiy 8; Pindyurin Vasily 14; and © Getty Images: David Redfern/Redferns 19; Michael Putland 33; Rob Verhorst/Redferns 69; Fin Costello/Redferns 85; Larry Hulst/Michael Ochs Archives 127; Kevin Mazur Archive 1/WireImage 149.

Every effort has been made to contact copyright holders. We apologize in advance for any omissions and would be pleased to insert the appropriate acknowledgement in subsequent editions of this publication.

Android is a trademark of Google Inc. Logic Pro, iPhone and iPad are either registered trademarks or trademarks of Apple Computer Inc. in the United States and/or other countries. Cubase is a registered trademark or trademark of Steinberg Media Technologies GmbH, a wholly owned subsidiary of Yamaha Corporation, in the United States and/or other countries. Nokia's product names are either trademarks or registered trademarks of Nokia. Nokia is a registered trademark of Nokia Corporation in the United States and/or other countries. Samsung and Galaxy S are both registered trademarks of Samsung Electronics America, Ltd. in the United States and/or other countries.

This book is an adaptation of How to Play Classic Riffs by Alan Brown & Jake Jackson, originally published in 2010.

Alan Brown (musical examples) is a former member of the Scottish National Orchestra. He now works as a freelance musician with several leading UK orchestras, and as a consultant in music and IT. Alan has had several compositions published, developed a set of music theory CD-Roms, co-written a series of bass guitar examination handbooks and worked on over 100 further titles.

Jake Jackson (author) is a writer and musician. He has created and contributed to over 25 practical music books, including Guitar Chords and How to Play Guitar. His music is available on iTunes, Amazon and Spotify amongst others.

Printed in China

Classic Riffs
An Introduction

A good sense of the types of riffs already out there will give a good foundation for making your own great music. Divided by type, the riffs in this book embody the styles of guitar heroes, delivering the essence of their technique and the melodic and rhythmic character of their creations.

1. **Basics** introduces classic riffs, with advice on creating your own and a handy reference of chord charts for all the chords that appear in this book.

2. **Blues** presents riff styles from Robert Johnson to Stevie Ray Vaughan, with the likes of B.B. King and John Lee Hooker thrown in for good measure.

3. **Early Rock** takes you from the honey-smooth perfection of Eric Clapton's riff style to the 'King of Riff' himself, Keith Richards, including other greats such as Chuck Berry, Dave Davies and Pete Townshend.

4. **Prog Rock** looks at the very best of progressive, experimental and psychedelic riff styles, including those by Queen, Pink Floyd and Jimi Hendrix.

5. **Hard Rock** is the section to go to for the intricate and intoxicating styles driving the sound of Guns N' Roses, Black Sabbath, AC/DC, Van Halen, Metallica, Aerosmith, Joe Satriani, Jimmy Page and more.

6. **Soft Rock** includes smoother, tuneful riffs bordering on funk and pop, like those by The Beatles, Dire Straits and The Shadows.

7. **Indie Rock** showcases riff styles from the more alternative and punk rock scene, including those by Kurt Cobain, Tom Morello, John Frusciante, Tom Verlaine and others.

START
HERE

BASICS

BLUES

EARLY
ROCK

PROG
ROCK

HARD
ROCK

SOFT
ROCK

INDIE
ROCK

The Diagrams
A Quick Guide

Each riff is notated in both traditional musical notation and guitar tablature. This book assumes a certain amount of musical knowledge, although diagram explanations are below.

First off, a few things to look out for when using the stave notation:

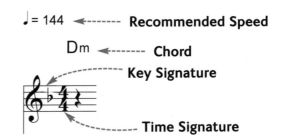

♩ = 144 ◄-------- **Recommended Speed**

Dm ◄-------- **Chord**

Key Signature

Time Signature

TAB Notation

Some guitarists prefer to use tablature (called TAB) instead of staves. The six lines represent the six strings of the guitar, from the high E string to the low E string, and the numbers represent the frets that produce the notes. A zero indicates that the string is played open. In the below example, the first C is played on the 5th string – the A string – by holding down the third fret along.

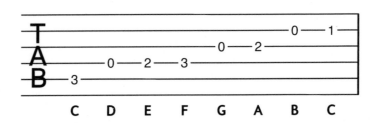

C   D   E   F   G   A   B   C

FREE ACCESS on iPhone & Android etc, using any free QR code app

Scan to **HEAR** the C major chord, and access the full library of scales and chords on flametreemusic.com

Chord Diagrams

The Strings: The bass E appears on the left (6th string).

The top E is on the right (1st string).

The top E is the E above **middle C** on the piano.

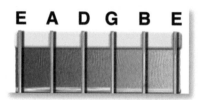

E A D G B E

Fingerings: ❶ is the index finger   ❷ is the middle finger

❸ is the ring finger   ❹ is the little finger

String isn't
played

Open string
position

Nut at the top
of the neck

The 1st
fret*

Finger position
for the notes

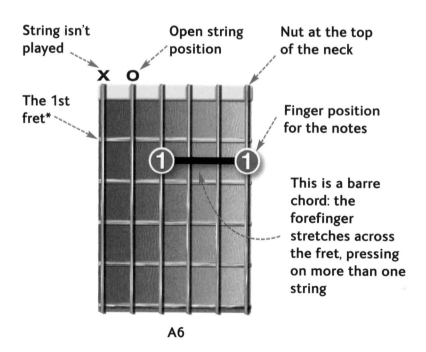

This is a barre
chord: the
forefinger
stretches across
the fret, pressing
on more than one
string

A6

*When the chord position isn't as close to the nut, a number to the left indicates the changed location on the fretboard. E.g. a '2' means the diagram starts from the 2nd fret rather than the 1st.

FREE ACCESS on iPhone & Android
etc, using any free QR code app

Scan to **HEAR** the C major chord, and
access the full library of scales and
chords on flametreemusic.com

START
HERE

BASICS

BLUES

EARLY
ROCK

PROG
ROCK

HARD
ROCK

SOFT
ROCK

INDIE
ROCK

The Sound Links
Another Quick Guide

Requirements: a camera and internet-ready smartphone (e.g. **iPhone**, any **Android** phone (e.g. **Samsung Galaxy**), **Nokia Lumia**, or **camera-enabled tablet** such as the **iPad Mini**). The best result is achieved using a WIFI connection.

1. Download any **free QR code reader**. An app store search will reveal a great many of these, so obviously it's best to go with the ones with the highest ratings and don't be afraid to try a few before you settle on the one that works best for you. Tapmedia's QR Reader app is good, or ATT Scanner (used below) or QR Media. Some of the free apps have ads, which can be annoying.

2. On your smartphone, open the app and **scan** the **QR code** at the base of any particular page.

FREE ACCESS on iPhone & Android etc, using any free QR code app

Scan to HEAR the C major chord, and access the full library of scales and chords on flametreemusic.com

7

3. Scanning the code will bring you to the C major chord, and from there you can access and hear the complete library of scales and chords.

FREE ACCESS on iPhone & Android etc, using any free QR code app

Scan to HEAR the C major chord, and access the full library of scales and chords on flametreemusic.com

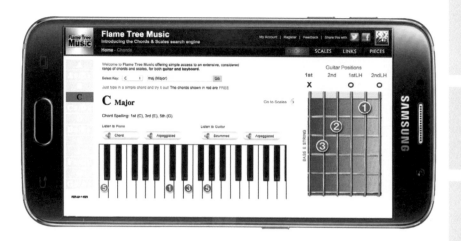

4. Use the drop down menu to choose from **20 scales** or 12 **free chords** (50 with subscription) per key.

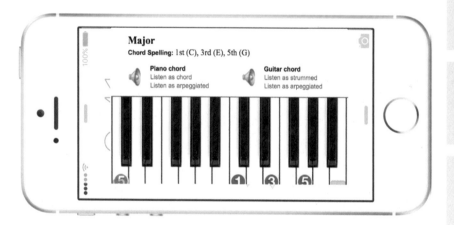

5. Click the sounds! Both piano and guitar audio is provided. This is particularly helpful when you're playing with others.

The QR codes give you direct access to chords and scales. You can access a much wider range of chords if you register and subscribe.

FREE ACCESS on iPhone & Android etc, using any free QR code app

Scan to **HEAR** the C major chord, and access the full library of scales and chords on flametreemusic.com

START HERE

BASICS

BLUES

EARLY ROCK

PROG ROCK

HARD ROCK

SOFT ROCK

INDIE ROCK

Riffs

A riff is a short musical phrase that is repeated many times throughout a song. It is often confused with a lick, which is a recognizable component of a solo or lead part that may crop up only once or twice. The repetitive, bold sound of a riff, though, is what 'hooks' you into the song.

Riffs also provide a good background for improvisation – so are likely to be consistent and predictable rather than something that will vary. In fact, seemingly complex riffs are often based on simple harmonic structures, so they can be mastered much quicker than whole songs. Remember, though, that playing chord riffs will inevitably involve the need for some fast chord changes. When practising, it is best to start slow and build up speed once you've perfected the movements. Try also to be aware of what chords you are passing through when playing the riffs in this book, as that will help you make more sense of the patterns.

START HERE

BASICS

BLUES

EARLY ROCK

PROG ROCK

HARD ROCK

SOFT ROCK

INDIE ROCK

FREE ACCESS on iPhone & Android etc, using any free QR code app

Scan to **HEAR** the C major chord, and access the full library of scales and chords on flametreemusic.com

Creating Your Own Classic Riffs

An effective riff is compelling, scratching at your memory for days. The riffs in this book are designed to give you a flavour of the types of styles already out there, to hopefully inspire you to experiment a little with the sounds and come up with your own. Here are a few features that usually appear in classic riffs.

Chords

Using chords to play riffs will nearly always result in a stronger and more memorable riff than those that use only single notes. When creating riffs with chords, you'll normally need to use more than one chord per measure in order to give a sense of movement. This might mean changing quickly to a totally different chord, or the riffs may just consist of chordal variations (such as major chords changing to suspended chords).

Rests

Rests between chords help add a well-defined rhythm to a riff, giving it musical shape and character. Place the strumming hand against the strings when you wish to mute them.

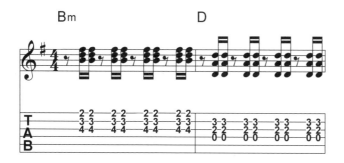

START HERE

BASICS

BLUES

EARLY ROCK

PROG ROCK

HARD ROCK

SOFT ROCK

INDIE ROCK

FREE ACCESS on iPhone & Android etc, using any free QR code app

Scan to **HEAR** the C major chord, and access the full library of scales and chords on flametreemusic.com

START
HERE

BASICS

BLUES

EARLY
ROCK

PROG
ROCK

HARD
ROCK

SOFT
ROCK

INDIE
ROCK

Separating Strings

An effective technique for chord riffing is to separate the bass and treble strings when a chord is played. This creates a piano-like effect, with the bass part clearly separated from the treble.

Using Power Chords

Power chords – consisting of just the root and fifth notes – are often used in riffs as the sound is tighter and better defined than when strumming all the strings of a complete chord shape.

Arpeggios

An arpeggio is a broken chord in which the notes of the chord are played individually (rather than strummed simultaneously). As the notes of each arpeggio are taken from their chord equivalent, they can sound very tuneful and add colour to the chordal accompaniment.

FREE ACCESS on iPhone & Android etc, using any free QR code app

Scan to **HEAR** the C major chord, and access the full library of scales and chords on flametreemusic.com

Adding Single Notes

Chord riffs do not need to consist exclusively of chords: adding an occasional single note, particularly an open bass string, can add variety to a riff and often make it easier to play.

Pentatonic Scales

The pentatonic scale is a popular scale for improvisation, as it has fewer notes that the standard 7-note scales, so there is less chance of any of the notes clashing with the accompanying chords. Below is the basic structure for the major and minor pentatonic scales, which can be applied to all keys and used as a good basis for riffs.

C Major

C Minor

Scan to **HEAR** the C major chord, and access the full library of scales and chords on flametreemusic.com

Chord Charts

As a quick reference, over the following pages we've listed chord charts for all the chords that appear in this book's riffs. You can hear how each chord sounds, and how each note in the chord sounds, at **flametreemusic.com**.

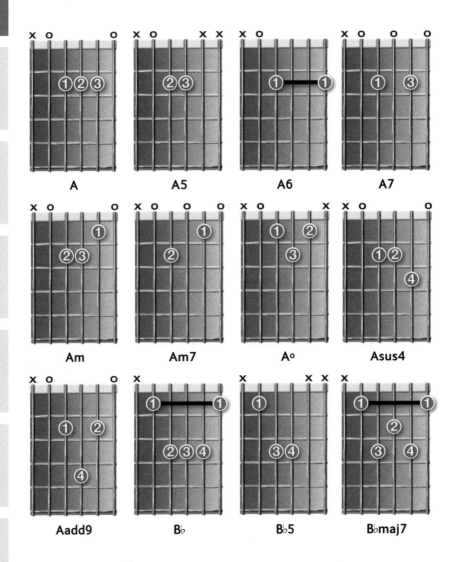

A   A5   A6   A7

Am   Am7   A°   Asus4

Aadd9   B♭   B♭5   B♭maj7

Scan to **HEAR** the C major chord, and access the full library of scales and chords on flametreemusic.com

FREE ACCESS on iPhone & Android etc, using any free QR code app

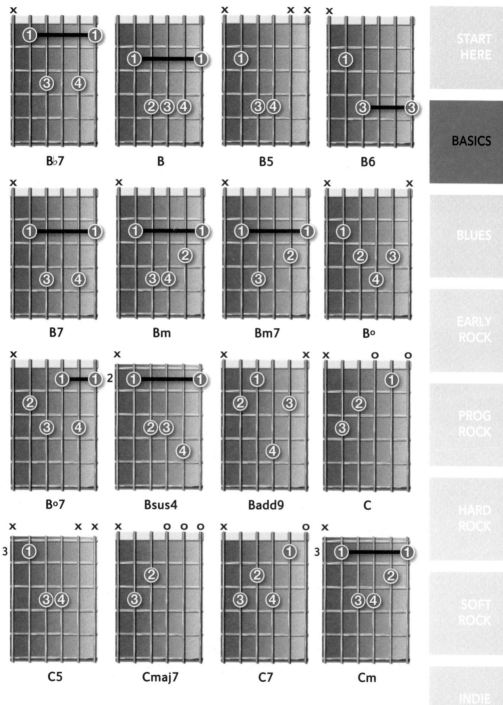

B♭7	B	B5	B6
B7	Bm	Bm7	B°
B°7	Bsus4	Badd9	C
C5	Cmaj7	C7	Cm

START HERE

BASICS

BLUES

EARLY ROCK

PROG ROCK

HARD ROCK

SOFT ROCK

INDIE ROCK

FREE ACCESS on iPhone & Android etc, using any free QR code app

Scan to **HEAR** the C major chord, and access the full library of scales and chords on flametreemusic.com

START
HERE

BASICS

BLUES

EARLY
ROCK

PROG
ROCK

HARD
ROCK

SOFT
ROCK

INDIE
ROCK

FREE ACCESS on iPhone & Android
etc, using any free QR code app

Scan to **HEAR** the C major chord, and
access the full library of scales and
chords on flametreemusic.com

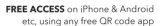

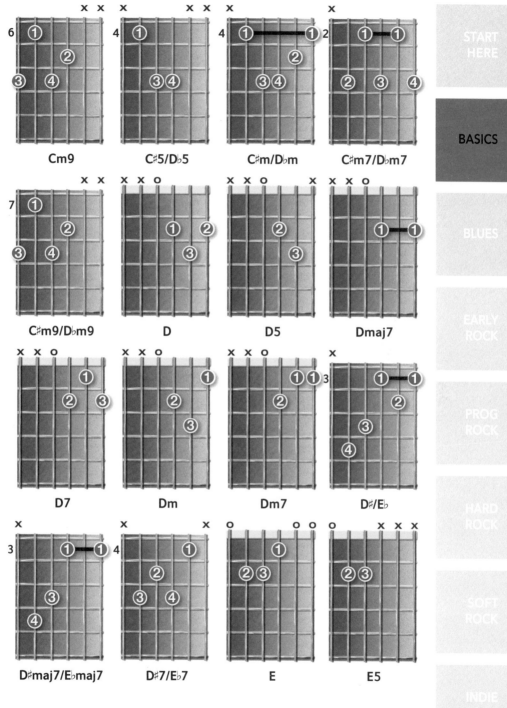

Cm9 C♯5/D♭5 C♯m/D♭m C♯m7/D♭m7

C♯m9/D♭m9 D D5 Dmaj7

D7 Dm Dm7 D♯/E♭

D♯maj7/E♭maj7 D♯7/E♭7 E E5

START HERE

BASICS

BLUES

EARLY ROCK

PROG ROCK

HARD ROCK

SOFT ROCK

INDIE ROCK

FREE ACCESS on iPhone & Android etc, using any free QR code app

Scan to **HEAR** the C major chord, and access the full library of scales and chords on flametreemusic.com

START
HERE

BASICS

BLUES

EARLY
ROCK

PROG
ROCK

HARD
ROCK

SOFT
ROCK

INDIE
ROCK

E6

E7

Em

Em7

E°

Esus4

F

F5

Fmaj7

F7

Fm

F#

F#5

F#6

F#m

F#m7

FREE ACCESS on iPhone & Android
etc, using any free QR code app

Scan to **HEAR** the C major chord, and
access the full library of scales and
chords on flametreemusic.com

16

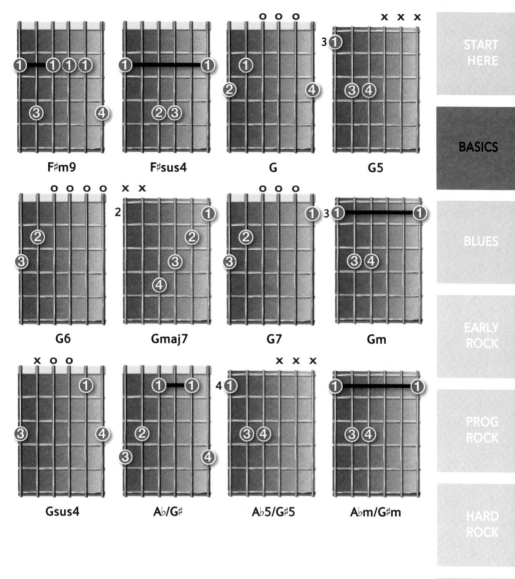

If you'd like to use chords that aren't listed here, you can head to **flametreemusic.com** for a comprehensive set of chord charts. There, you can also hear how each chord sounds, making it easier for you to play and experiment with your own riffs.

Scan to **HEAR** the C major chord, and access the full library of scales and chords on flametreemusic.com

START
HERE

BASICS

BLUES

EARLY
ROCK

PROG
ROCK

HARD
ROCK

SOFT
ROCK

INDIE
ROCK

Blues

The following sections chart the progression of the rock riff from its early roots through to its most popular forms today. First up: the Blues.

Sometimes the blues can seem hard to get into because the crackly, original recordings seem distant or inaccessible. The blues, however, encompass an enduring range of riffing techniques within the 12-bar straitjacket, and the pioneers of the style encouraged a musical language that still allows any two guitar players, of any ability, to come together and make a great sound. The simplicity and downright dirtiness of Chicago blues pioneer Muddy Water's 'Mannish Boy' or the unfettered freedom of John Lee Hooker's 'Boogie Chillen'' – blowsy and loose, somewhere between a laugh, a cough and a whoop – inspired a generation of British white boys in the early Sixties to borrow the riffs and take the music to a new generation. For many though, the originals are still the best.

As you play through the riffs in this book you will notice the same sorts of features cropping up for particular styles: in the Blues section, for example, syncopation is a common feature, giving the rhythms a 'swung' feel.

This section includes riffs in the style of the following artists:

- John Lee Hooker
- Elmore James
- Robert Johnson
- B.B. King
- Stevie Ray Vaughan (Double Trouble)
- Muddy Waters

FREE ACCESS on iPhone & Android etc, using any free QR code app

Scan to **HEAR** the C major chord, and access the full library of scales and chords on flametreemusic.com

START HERE

BASICS

BLUES

EARLY ROCK

PROG ROCK

HARD ROCK

SOFT ROCK

INDIE ROCK

FREE ACCESS on iPhone & Android etc, using any free QR code app

Scan to **HEAR** the C major chord, and access the full library of scales and chords on flametreemusic.com

John Lee Hooker

START
HERE

BASICS

BLUES

EARLY
ROCK

PROG
ROCK

HARD
ROCK

SOFT
ROCK

INDIE
ROCK

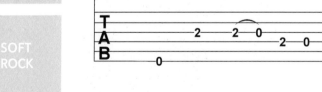

Scan to **HEAR** the C major chord, and
access the full library of scales and
chords on flametreemusic.com

START
HERE

A

E

EARLY
ROCK

PROG
ROCK

HARD
ROCK

SOFT
ROCK

INDIE
ROCK

FREE ACCESS on iPhone & Android
etc, using any free QR code app

Scan to **HEAR** the C major chord, and
access the full library of scales and
chords on flametreemusic.com

Elmore James

START
HERE

BASICS

BLUES

EARLY
ROCK

PROG
ROCK

HARD
ROCK

SOFT
ROCK

INDIE
ROCK

♩ = 116

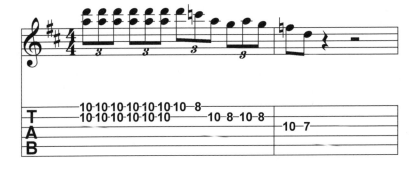

Scan to **HEAR** the C major chord, and access the full library of scales and chords on flametreemusic.com

START
HERE

BASICS

BLUES

EARLY
ROCK

PROG
ROCK

HARD
ROCK

SOFT
ROCK

INDIE
ROCK

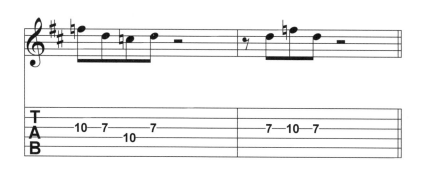

FREE ACCESS on iPhone & Android
etc, using any free QR code app

Scan to **HEAR** the C major chord, and
access the full library of scales and
chords on flametreemusic.com

Robert Johnson

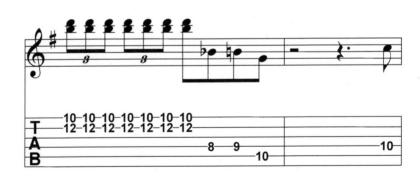

Scan to **HEAR** the C major chord, and access the full library of scales and chords on flametreemusic.com

START
HERE

BASICS

BLUES

EARLY
ROCK

PROG
ROCK

HARD
ROCK

SOFT
ROCK

INDIE
ROCK

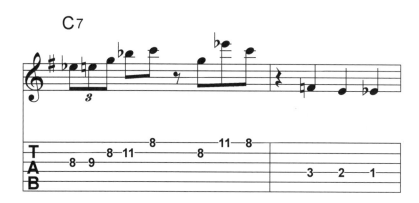

FREE ACCESS on iPhone & Android
etc, using any free QR code app

Scan to **HEAR** the C major chord, and
access the full library of scales and
chords on flametreemusic.com

B.B. King

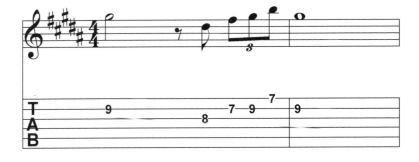

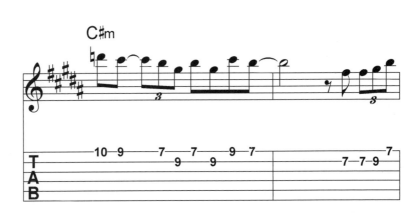

FREE ACCESS on iPhone & Android
etc, using any free QR code app

Scan to **HEAR** the C major chord, and
access the full library of scales and
chords on flametreemusic.com

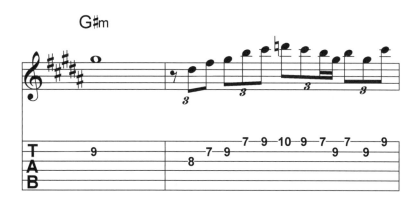

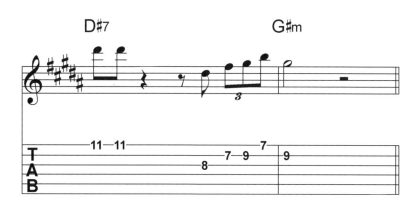

Stevie Ray Vaughan
(Double Trouble)

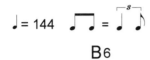

Scan to **HEAR** the C major chord, and access the full library of scales and chords on flametreemusic.com

START HERE

BASICS

BLUES

EARLY ROCK

PROG ROCK

HARD ROCK

SOFT ROCK

INDIE ROCK

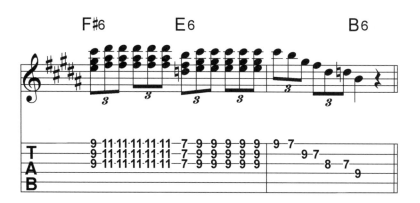

FREE ACCESS on iPhone & Android
etc, using any free QR code app

Scan to **HEAR** the C major chord, and
access the full library of scales and
chords on flametreemusic.com

29

Muddy Waters

START
HERE

BASICS

BLUES

EARLY
ROCK

PROG
ROCK

HARD
ROCK

SOFT
ROCK

INDIE
ROCK

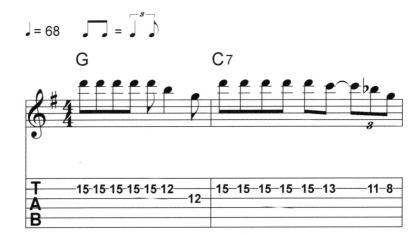

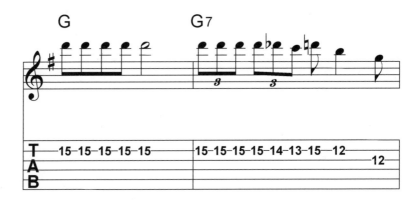

Scan to **HEAR** the C major chord, and
access the full library of scales and
chords on flametreemusic.com

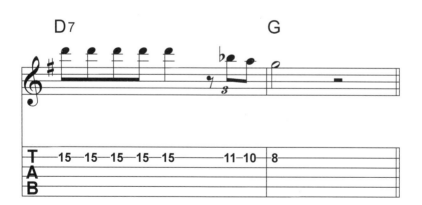

Scan to **HEAR** the C major chord, and access the full library of scales and chords on flametreemusic.com

START
HERE

BASICS

BLUES

EARLY
ROCK

PROG
ROCK

HARD
ROCK

SOFT
ROCK

INDIE
ROCK

Rock'n'Roll, R&B & Blues Rock

Chuck Berry, rock'n'roll's first true king, dragged the blues into an electric era that filled the dancehalls and clubs with loud and joyful music.

Dramatically, in the 1950s the blues was thrust together with a restless teenage generation and created a demon child: rock'n'roll. Curiously though, it was the British blues boom of the Sixties that secured the survival of rock and blues with Eric Clapton, Jeff Beck and Keith Richards transforming their own love of the blues into a lasting musical form.

This section includes riffs in the style of the following artists:

- Jeff Beck (Yardbirds)
- Chuck Berry
- Dickey Betts (The Allman Brothers Band)
- Eric Clapton
- Eddie Cochran
- Dick Dale
- Dave Davies (The Kinks)
- Duane Eddy
- Billy Gibbons (ZZ Top)
- Peter Green (Fleetwood Mac)
- Buddy Holly
- Gary Moore
- Keith Richards (The Rolling Stones)
- Francis Rossi & Rick Parfitt (Status Quo)
- Carlos Santana (Santana)
- George Thorogood (George Thorogood & The Destroyers)
- Pete Townshend (The Who)

FREE ACCESS on iPhone & Android etc, using any free QR code app

Scan to **HEAR** the C major chord, and access the full library of scales and chords on flametreemusic.com

START
HERE

BASICS

BLUES

EARLY
ROCK

PROG
ROCK

HARD
ROCK

SOFT
ROCK

INDIE
ROCK

FREE ACCESS on iPhone & Android
etc, using any free QR code app

Scan to **HEAR** the C major chord, and
access the full library of scales and
chords on flametreemusic.com

Jeff Beck
(Yardbirds)

START
HERE

BASICS

BLUES

EARLY
ROCK

PROG
ROCK

HARD
ROCK

SOFT
ROCK

INDIE
ROCK

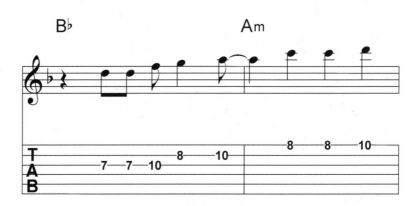

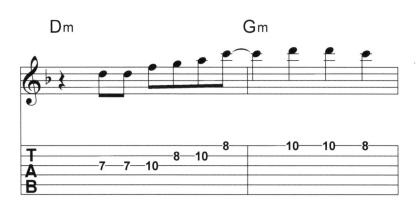

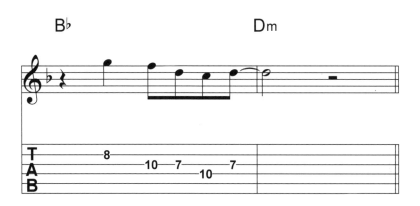

FREE ACCESS on iPhone & Android etc, using any free QR code app

Scan to **HEAR** the C major chord, and access the full library of scales and chords on flametreemusic.com

Chuck Berry

START
HERE

BASICS

BLUES

EARLY
ROCK

PROG
ROCK

HARD
ROCK

SOFT
ROCK

INDIE
ROCK

Scan to **HEAR** the C major chord, and
access the full library of scales and
chords on flametreemusic.com

FREE ACCESS on iPhone & Android etc, using any free QR code app

Scan to **HEAR** the C major chord, and access the full library of scales and chords on flametreemusic.com

Dickey Betts
(The Allman Brothers Band)

START
HERE

BASICS

BLUES

EARLY
ROCK

PROG
ROCK

HARD
ROCK

SOFT
ROCK

INDIE
ROCK

♩ = 100

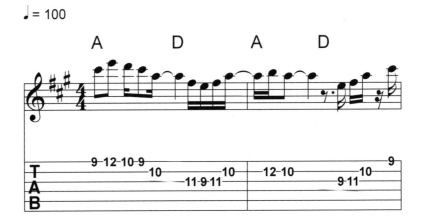

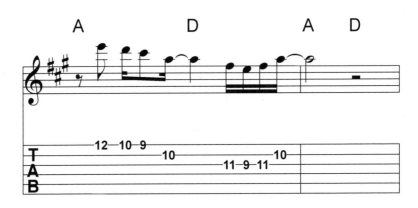

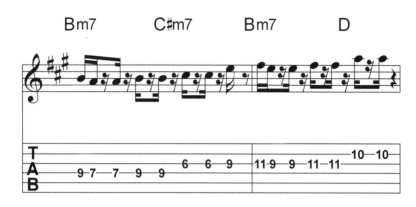

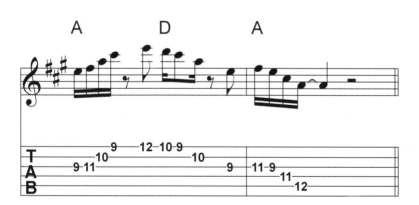

FREE ACCESS on iPhone & Android etc, using any free QR code app

Scan to **HEAR** the C major chord, and access the full library of scales and chords on flametreemusic.com

Eric Clapton

START
HERE

BASICS

BLUES

EARLY
ROCK

PROG
ROCK

HARD
ROCK

SOFT
ROCK

INDIE
ROCK

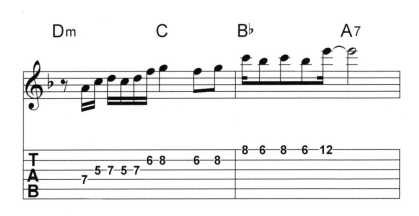

Scan to **HEAR** the C major chord, and
access the full library of scales and
chords on flametreemusic.com

START
HERE

BASICS

BLUES

EARLY
ROCK

PROG
ROCK

HARD
ROCK

SOFT
ROCK

INDIE
ROCK

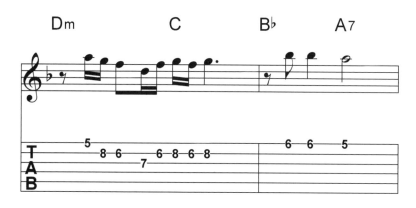

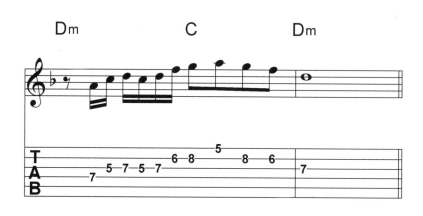

FREE ACCESS on iPhone & Android
etc, using any free QR code app

Scan to **HEAR** the C major chord, and
access the full library of scales and
chords on flametreemusic.com

41

Eddie Cochran

START HERE

BASICS

BLUES

EARLY ROCK

PROG ROCK

HARD ROCK

SOFT ROCK

INDIE ROCK

♩ = 144

G

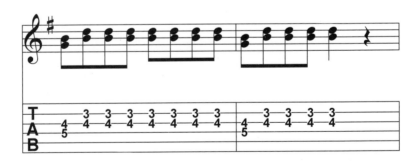

START
HERE

BASICS

BLUES

EARLY
ROCK

PROG
ROCK

HARD
ROCK

SOFT
ROCK

INDIE
ROCK

Dick Dale

Scan to **HEAR** the C major chord, and access the full library of scales and chords on flametreemusic.com

START HERE

BASICS

BLUES

EARLY ROCK

PROG ROCK

HARD ROCK

SOFT ROCK

INDIE ROCK

START
HERE

BASICS

BLUES

EARLY
ROCK

PROG
ROCK

HARD
ROCK

SOFT
ROCK

INDIE
ROCK

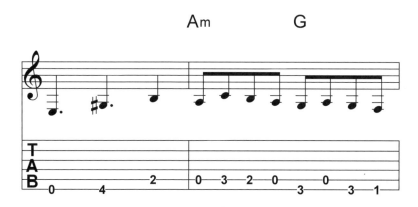

Scan to **HEAR** the C major chord, and
access the full library of scales and
chords on flametreemusic.com

Dave Davies
(The Kinks)

START
HERE

BASICS

BLUES

EARLY
ROCK

PROG
ROCK

HARD
ROCK

SOFT
ROCK

INDIE
ROCK

Scan to **HEAR** the C major chord, and access the full library of scales and chords on flametreemusic.com

A

Scan to **HEAR** the C major chord, and access the full library of scales and chords on flametreemusic.com

START HERE

BASICS

BLUES

EARLY ROCK

PROG ROCK

HARD ROCK

SOFT ROCK

INDIE ROCK

Duane Eddy

START HERE

BASICS

BLUES

EARLY ROCK

PROG ROCK

HARD ROCK

SOFT ROCK

INDIE ROCK

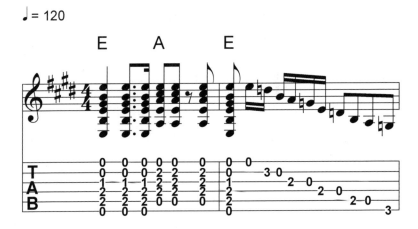

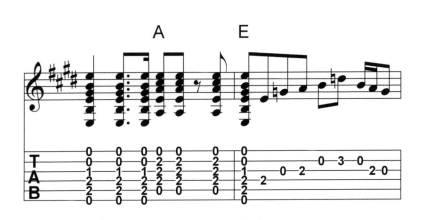

Scan to **HEAR** the C major chord, and access the full library of scales and chords on flametreemusic.com

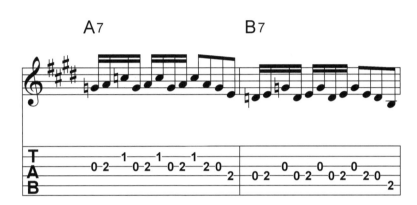

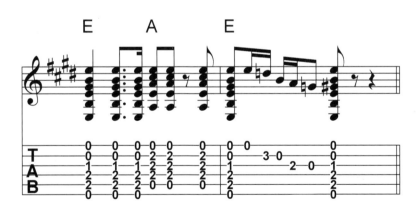

Scan to **HEAR** the C major chord, and access the full library of scales and chords on flametreemusic.com

START HERE

BASICS

BLUES

EARLY ROCK

PROG ROCK

HARD ROCK

SOFT ROCK

INDIE ROCK

Billy Gibbons
(ZZ Top)

START
HERE

BASICS

BLUES

EARLY
ROCK

PROG
ROCK

HARD
ROCK

SOFT
ROCK

INDIE
ROCK

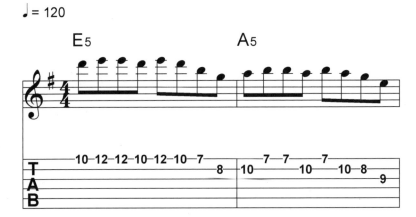

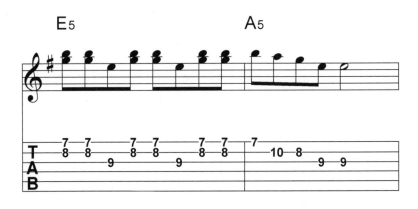

FREE ACCESS on iPhone & Android etc, using any free QR code app

Scan to **HEAR** the C major chord, and access the full library of scales and chords on flametreemusic.com

START HERE

BASICS

BLUES

EARLY ROCK

PROG ROCK

HARD ROCK

SOFT ROCK

INDIE ROCK

FREE ACCESS on iPhone & Android etc, using any free QR code app

Scan to **HEAR** the C major chord, and access the full library of scales and chords on flametreemusic.com

Peter Green
(Fleetwood Mac)

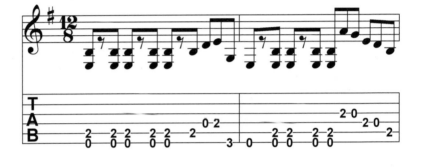

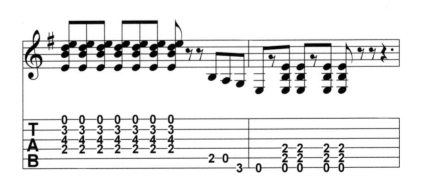

START
HERE

BASICS

BLUES

EARLY
ROCK

PROG
ROCK

HARD
ROCK

SOFT
ROCK

INDIE
ROCK

FREE ACCESS on iPhone & Android
etc, using any free QR code app

Scan to **HEAR** the C major chord, and
access the full library of scales and
chords on flametreemusic.com

START HERE

BASICS

BLUES

EARLY ROCK

PROG ROCK

HARD ROCK

SOFT ROCK

INDIE ROCK

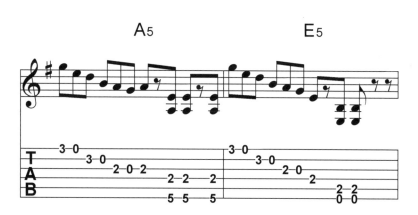

FREE ACCESS on iPhone & Android
etc, using any free QR code app

Scan to **HEAR** the C major chord, and
access the full library of scales and
chords on flametreemusic.com

Buddy Holly

FREE ACCESS on iPhone & Android
etc, using any free QR code app

Scan to **HEAR** the C major chord, and
access the full library of scales and
chords on flametreemusic.com

**EARLY
ROCK**

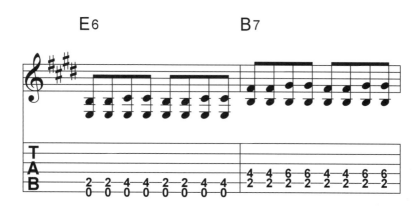

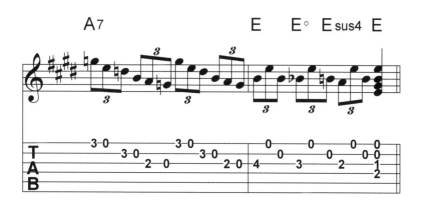

Gary Moore

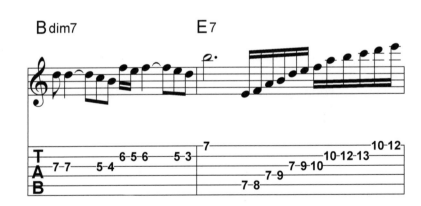

Scan to **HEAR** the C major chord, and access the full library of scales and chords on flametreemusic.com

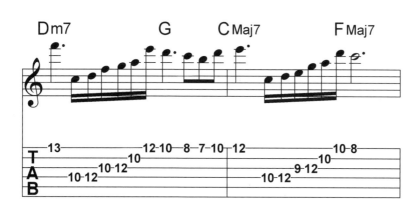

START HERE

BASICS

BLUES

EARLY ROCK

PROG ROCK

HARD ROCK

SOFT ROCK

INDIE ROCK

FREE ACCESS on iPhone & Android etc, using any free QR code app

Scan to **HEAR** the C major chord, and access the full library of scales and chords on flametreemusic.com

Keith Richards
(The Rolling Stones)

START HERE

BASICS

BLUES

EARLY ROCK

PROG ROCK

HARD ROCK

SOFT ROCK

INDIE ROCK

♩ = 108

A

B

FREE ACCESS on iPhone & Android
etc, using any free QR code app

Scan to **HEAR** the C major chord, and
access the full library of scales and
chords on flametreemusic.com

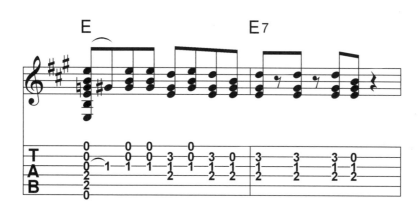

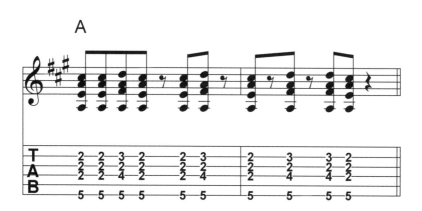

FREE ACCESS on iPhone & Android
etc, using any free QR code app

Scan to HEAR the C major chord, and
access the full library of scales and
chords on flametreemusic.com

Francis Rossi & Rick Parfitt
(Status Quo)

START
HERE

BASICS

BLUES

EARLY
ROCK

PROG
ROCK

HARD
ROCK

SOFT
ROCK

INDIE
ROCK

FREE ACCESS on iPhone & Android
etc, using any free QR code app

Scan to **HEAR** the C major chord, and
access the full library of scales and
chords on flametreemusic.com

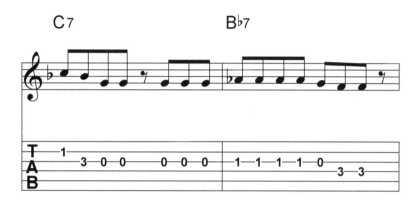

FREE ACCESS on iPhone & Android etc, using any free QR code app

Scan to **HEAR** the C major chord, and access the full library of scales and chords on flametreemusic.com

Carlos Santana
(Santana)

START
HERE

BASICS

BLUES

EARLY
ROCK

PROG
ROCK

HARD
ROCK

SOFT
ROCK

INDIE
ROCK

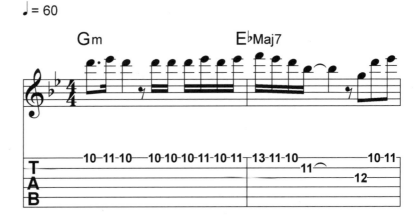

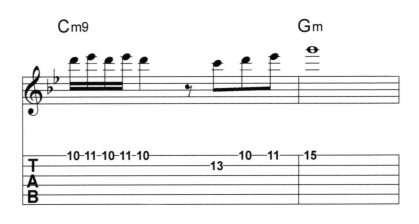

FREE ACCESS on iPhone & Android
etc, using any free QR code app

Scan to HEAR the C major chord, and
access the full library of scales and
chords on flametreemusic.com

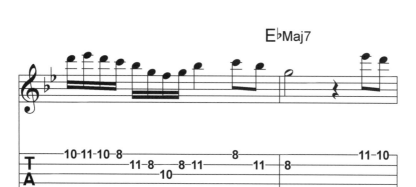

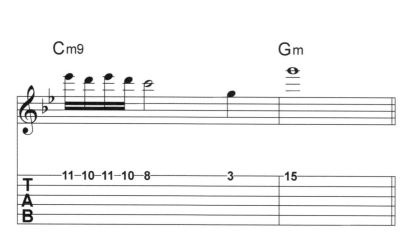

START
HERE

BASICS

BLUES

EARLY
ROCK

PROG
ROCK

HARD
ROCK

SOFT
ROCK

INDIE
ROCK

FREE ACCESS on iPhone & Android
etc, using any free QR code app

Scan to **HEAR** the C major chord, and
access the full library of scales and
chords on flametreemusic.com

George Thorogood
(George Thorogood & The Destroyers)

♩. = 112

G₅

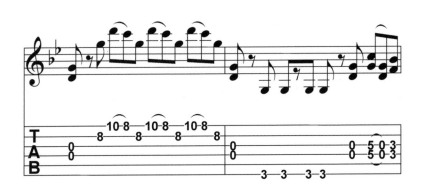

Scan to **HEAR** the C major chord, and
access the full library of scales and
chords on flametreemusic.com

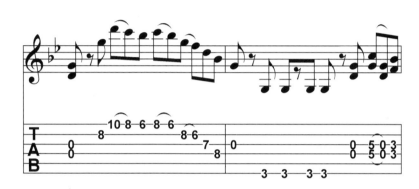

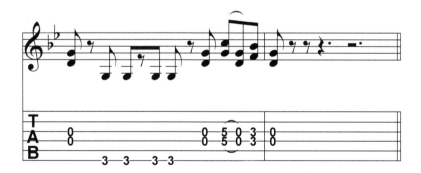

FREE ACCESS on iPhone & Android
etc, using any free QR code app

Scan to **HEAR** the C major chord, and
access the full library of scales and
chords on flametreemusic.com

Pete Townshend
(The Who)

START
HERE

BASICS

BLUES

EARLY
ROCK

PROG
ROCK

HARD
ROCK

SOFT
ROCK

INDIE
ROCK

START HERE

BASICS

BLUES

EARLY ROCK

PROG ROCK

HARD ROCK

SOFT ROCK

INDIE ROCK

Scan to **HEAR** the C major chord, and access the full library of scales and chords on flametreemusic.com

START
HERE

BASICS

BLUES

EARLY
ROCK

PROG
ROCK

HARD
ROCK

SOFT
ROCK

INDIE
ROCK

Psychedelic, Prog & Experimental Rock

In the late Sixties and early Seventies, some artists were tiring of the pop-rock sounds and their bluesy roots.

The new rock generations started to experiment with different musical traditions and the changes in recording and sound technology brought in new guitar pedal effects and loops. The dominance of the tight three-minute single was also challenged by a wide range of musicians, led in fact by pop kings like *The Beatles*, with their own psychedelic offerings. From these roots grew the spacey rock of early *Pink Floyd*, the dense articulations of *King Crimson* and Steve Howe's spiky, trebly musings in *Yes*. Rock's riffs grew longer, more challenging and reached a zenith of creating the majestic concoctions of Brian May's scintillating operatic style. For some, this way led to divine madness, but for others it grew into a gigantic pomposity, which would eventually be pricked by the onslaught of punk.

This section includes riffs in the style of the following artists:

- Adrian Belew (King Crimson)
- David Gilmour (Pink Floyd)
- Steve Hackett (Genesis)
- Jimi Hendrix (The Jimi Hendrix Experience)
- Steve Howe (Yes)
- Robby Krieger (The Doors)
- Brian May (Queen)

FREE ACCESS on iPhone & Android etc, using any free QR code app

Scan to **HEAR** the C major chord, and access the full library of scales and chords on flametreemusic.com

START HERE

BASICS

BLUES

EARLY ROCK

PROG ROCK

HARD ROCK

SOFT ROCK

INDIE ROCK

FREE ACCESS on iPhone & Android etc, using any free QR code app

Scan to **HEAR** the C major chord, and access the full library of scales and chords on flametreemusic.com

Adrian Belew
(King Crimson)

START
HERE

BASICS

BLUES

EARLY
ROCK

PROG
ROCK

HARD
ROCK

SOFT
ROCK

INDIE
ROCK

FREE ACCESS on iPhone & Android
etc, using any free QR code app

Scan to **HEAR** the C major chord, and
access the full library of scales and
chords on flametreemusic.com

Dm Gm Dm Gm Cm Fm Cm Fm

Cm

Scan to **HEAR** the C major chord, and
access the full library of scales and
chords on flametreemusic.com

START
HERE

BASICS

BLUES

EARLY
ROCK

PROG
ROCK

HARD
ROCK

SOFT
ROCK

INDIE
ROCK

David Gilmour
(Pink Floyd)

START
HERE

BASICS

BLUES

EARLY
ROCK

PROG
ROCK

HARD
ROCK

SOFT
ROCK

INDIE
ROCK

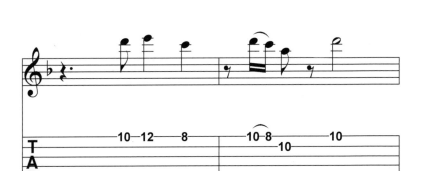

FREE ACCESS on iPhone & Android
etc, using any free QR code app

Scan to **HEAR** the C major chord, and
access the full library of scales and
chords on flametreemusic.com

START
HERE

BASICS

BLUES

EARLY
ROCK

PROG
ROCK

HARD
ROCK

SOFT
ROCK

INDIE
ROCK

Steve Hackett
(Genesis)

START
HERE

BASICS

BLUES

EARLY
ROCK

PROG
ROCK

HARD
ROCK

SOFT
ROCK

INDIE
ROCK

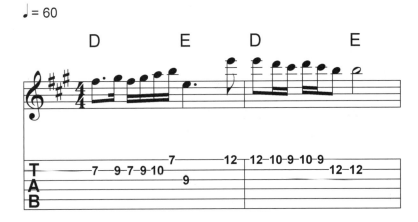

Scan to **HEAR** the C major chord, and access the full library of scales and chords on flametreemusic.com

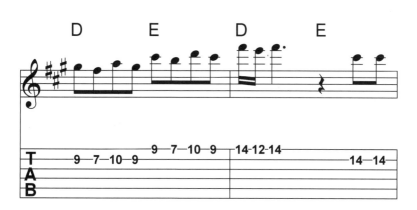

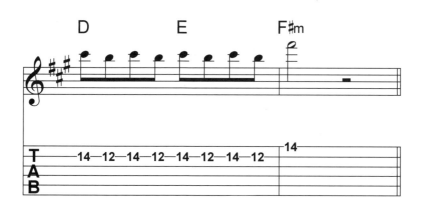

START HERE

BASICS

BLUES

EARLY ROCK

PROG ROCK

HARD ROCK

SOFT ROCK

INDIE ROCK

FREE ACCESS on iPhone & Android etc, using any free QR code app

Scan to **HEAR** the C major chord, and access the full library of scales and chords on flametreemusic.com

Jimi Hendrix
(The Jimi Hendrix Experience)

START
HERE

BASICS

BLUES

EARLY
ROCK

PROG
ROCK

HARD
ROCK

SOFT
ROCK

INDIE
ROCK

FREE ACCESS on iPhone & Android
etc, using any free QR code app

Scan to HEAR the C major chord, and
access the full library of scales and
chords on flametreemusic.com

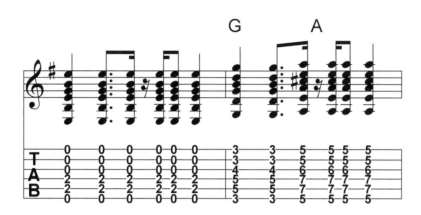

START
HERE

BASICS

BLUES

EARLY
ROCK

PROG
ROCK

HARD
ROCK

SOFT
ROCK

INDIE
ROCK

FREE ACCESS on iPhone & Android
etc, using any free QR code app

Scan to **HEAR** the C major chord, and
access the full library of scales and
chords on flametreemusic.com

Steve Howe
(Yes)

START
HERE

BASICS

BLUES

EARLY
ROCK

PROG
ROCK

HARD
ROCK

SOFT
ROCK

INDIE
ROCK

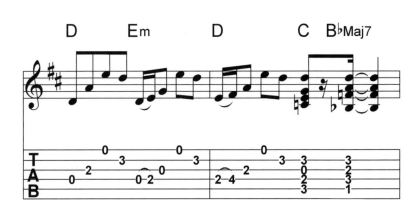

FREE ACCESS on iPhone & Android
etc, using any free QR code app

Scan to **HEAR** the C major chord, and
access the full library of scales and
chords on flametreemusic.com

START
HERE

BASICS

BLUES

EARLY
ROCK

PROG
ROCK

HARD
ROCK

SOFT
ROCK

INDIE
ROCK

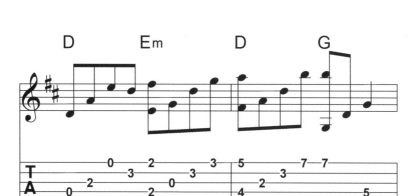

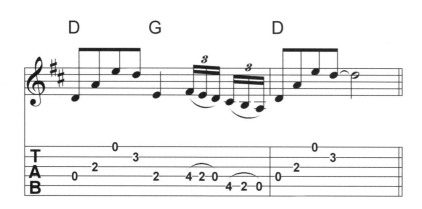

Scan to **HEAR** the C major chord, and
access the full library of scales and
chords on flametreemusic.com

Robby Krieger
(The Doors)

START
HERE

BASICS

BLUES

EARLY
ROCK

PROG
ROCK

HARD
ROCK

SOFT
ROCK

INDIE
ROCK

START
HERE

BASICS

BLUES

EARLY
ROCK

PROG
ROCK

HARD
ROCK

SOFT
ROCK

INDIE
ROCK

FREE ACCESS on iPhone & Android
etc, using any free QR code app

Scan to **HEAR** the C major chord, and
access the full library of scales and
chords on flametreemusic.com

Brian May
(Queen)

START
HERE

BASICS

BLUES

EARLY
ROCK

PROG
ROCK

HARD
ROCK

SOFT
ROCK

INDIE
ROCK

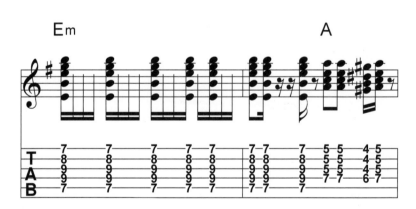

Scan to **HEAR** the C major chord, and
access the full library of scales and
chords on flametreemusic.com

START HERE

BASICS

BLUES

EARLY ROCK

PROG ROCK

HARD ROCK

SOFT ROCK

INDIE ROCK

Scan to **HEAR** the C major chord, and access the full library of scales and chords on flametreemusic.com

START
HERE

BASICS

BLUES

EARLY
ROCK

PROG
ROCK

HARD
ROCK

SOFT
ROCK

INDIE
ROCK

Hard Rock & Heavy Metal

While some artists loosened their grip on their blues rock roots, the quintessential rock band *Led Zeppelin* toughened the core of their sound.

Jimmy Page's ranting guitar and the screaming sonic boom of Robert Plant's vocals spawned a series of successors – from *Deep Purple*'s Ritchie Blackmore to Slash – until the ears of rock were bleeding, and loving it.

This section includes riffs in the style of the following artists:

- Ritchie Blackmore (Rainbow)
- Dimebag Darrell (Pantera)
- Scott Gorham & Brian Robertson (Thin Lizzy)
- James Hetfield (Metallica)
- Tony Iommi (Black Sabbath)
- Alex Lifeson (Rush)
- Yngwie Malmsteen
- Mick Mars (Mötley Crüe)
- Dave Murray & Adrian Smith (Iron Maiden)
- Dave Mustaine (Megadeth)
- Jimmy Page (Led Zeppelin)
- Joe Perry (Aerosmith)
- Randy Rhoads (Ozzy Osbourne)
- Uli Jon Roth (Scorpions)
- Richie Sambora (Bon Jovi)
- Joe Satriani
- Slash (Guns N' Roses)
- Glenn Tipton (Judas Priest)
- Eddie Van Halen (Van Halen)
- Angus & Malcolm Young (AC/DC)

FREE ACCESS on iPhone & Android etc, using any free QR code app

Scan to **HEAR** the C major chord, and access the full library of scales and chords on flametreemusic.com

START
HERE

BASICS

BLUES

EARLY
ROCK

PROG
ROCK

HARD
ROCK

SOFT
ROCK

INDIE
ROCK

FREE ACCESS on iPhone & Android etc,
using any free QR code app

Scan to **HEAR** the C major chord, and
access the full library of scales and
chords on flametreemusic.com

Ritchie Blackmore
(Rainbow)

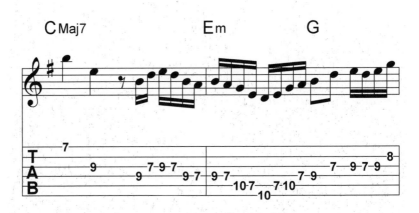

START
HERE

BASICS

BLUES

EARLY
ROCK

PROG
ROCK

HARD
ROCK

SOFT
ROCK

INDIE
ROCK

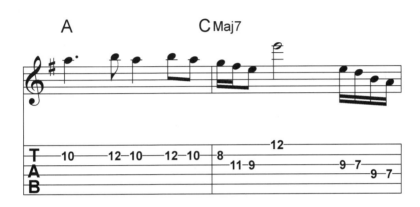

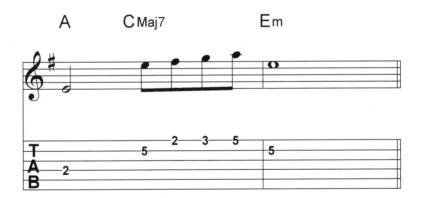

FREE ACCESS on iPhone & Android etc, using any free QR code app

Scan to **HEAR** the C major chord, and access the full library of scales and chords on flametreemusic.com

87

Dimebag Darrell
(Pantera)

FREE ACCESS on iPhone & Android
etc, using any free QR code app

Scan to **HEAR** the C major chord, and
access the full library of scales and
chords on flametreemusic.com

START
HERE

BASICS

BLUES

EARLY
ROCK

PROG
ROCK

HARD
ROCK

SOFT
ROCK

INDIE
ROCK

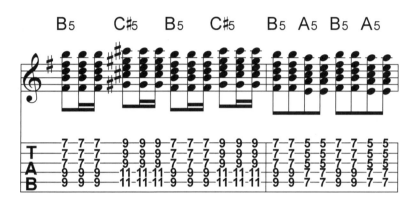

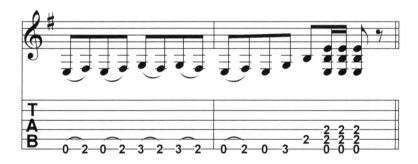

Scan to **HEAR** the C major chord, and access the full library of scales and chords on flametreemusic.com

Scott Gorham & Brian Robertson
(Thin Lizzy)

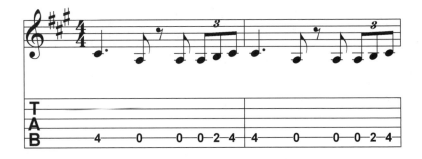

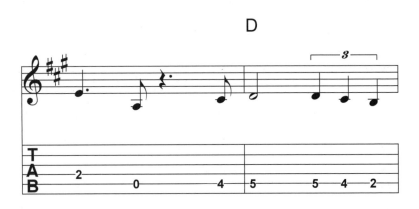

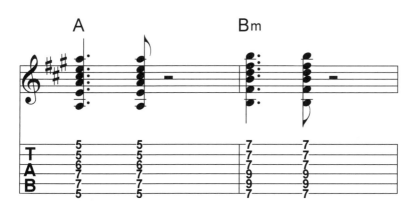

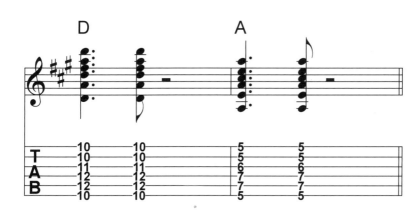

FREE ACCESS on iPhone & Android etc, using any free QR code app

Scan to **HEAR** the C major chord, and access the full library of scales and chords on flametreemusic.com

START
HERE

BASICS

BLUES

EARLY
ROCK

PROG
ROCK

HARD
ROCK

SOFT
ROCK

INDIE
ROCK

James Hetfield
(Metallica)

START
HERE

BASICS

BLUES

EARLY
ROCK

PROG
ROCK

HARD
ROCK

SOFT
ROCK

INDIE
ROCK

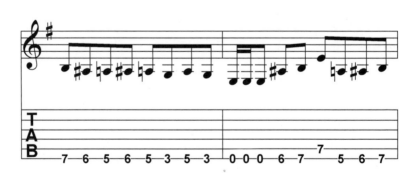

FREE ACCESS on iPhone & Android
etc, using any free QR code app

Scan to **HEAR** the C major chord, and
access the full library of scales and
chords on flametreemusic.com

START
HERE

BASICS

BLUES

EARLY
ROCK

PROG
ROCK

HARD
ROCK

SOFT
ROCK

INDIE
ROCK

FREE ACCESS on iPhone & Android etc, using any free QR code app

Scan to **HEAR** the C major chord, and access the full library of scales and chords on flametreemusic.com

Tony Iommi
(Black Sabbath)

START HERE

BASICS

BLUES

EARLY ROCK

PROG ROCK

HARD ROCK

SOFT ROCK

INDIE ROCK

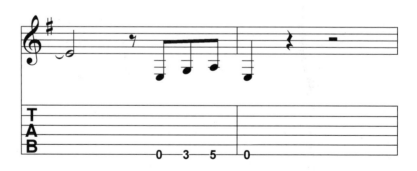

Scan to **HEAR** the C major chord, and access the full library of scales and chords on flametreemusic.com

Scan to **HEAR** the C major chord, and access the full library of scales and chords on flametreemusic.com

Alex Lifeson
(Rush)

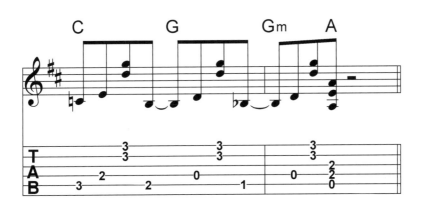

Scan to **HEAR** the C major chord, and
access the full library of scales and
chords on flametreemusic.com

START
HERE

BASICS

BLUES

EARLY
ROCK

PROG
ROCK

HARD
ROCK

SOFT
ROCK

INDIE
ROCK

Yngwie Malmsteen

START
HERE

BASICS

BLUES

EARLY
ROCK

PROG
ROCK

HARD
ROCK

SOFT
ROCK

INDIE
ROCK

♩ = 132

Scan to **HEAR** the C major chord, and
access the full library of scales and
chords on flametreemusic.com

START HERE

BASICS

BLUES

EARLY ROCK

PROG ROCK

HARD ROCK

SOFT ROCK

INDIE ROCK

FREE ACCESS on iPhone & Android etc, using any free QR code app

Scan to **HEAR** the C major chord, and access the full library of scales and chords on flametreemusic.com

Mick Mars
(Mötley Crüe)

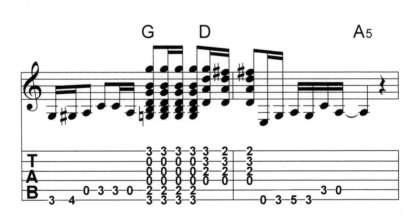

START HERE

BASICS

BLUES

EARLY ROCK

PROG ROCK

HARD ROCK

SOFT ROCK

INDIE ROCK

100

FREE ACCESS on iPhone & Android etc, using any free QR code app

Scan to **HEAR** the C major chord, and access the full library of scales and chords on flametreemusic.com

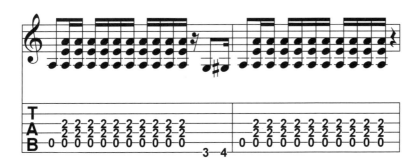

Scan to **HEAR** the C major chord, and
access the full library of scales and
chords on flametreemusic.com

START
HERE

BASICS

BLUES

EARLY
ROCK

PROG
ROCK

HARD
ROCK

SOFT
ROCK

INDIE
ROCK

Dave Murray & Adrian Smith
(Iron Maiden)

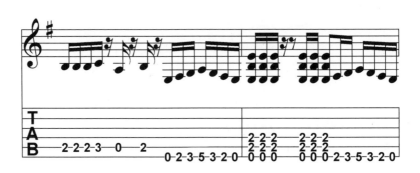

FREE ACCESS on iPhone & Android
etc, using any free QR code app

Scan to **HEAR** the C major chord, and
access the full library of scales and
chords on flametreemusic.com

START HERE

BASICS

BLUES

EARLY ROCK

PROG ROCK

HARD ROCK

SOFT ROCK

INDIE ROCK

START
HERE

BASICS

BLUES

EARLY
ROCK

PROG
ROCK

HARD
ROCK

SOFT
ROCK

INDIE
ROCK

FREE ACCESS on iPhone & Android etc,
using any free QR code app

Scan to **HEAR** the C major chord, and
access the full library of scales and
chords on flametreemusic.com

103

Dave Mustaine
(Megadeth)

START
HERE

BASICS

BLUES

EARLY
ROCK

PROG
ROCK

HARD
ROCK

SOFT
ROCK

INDIE
ROCK

♩ = 100

E5

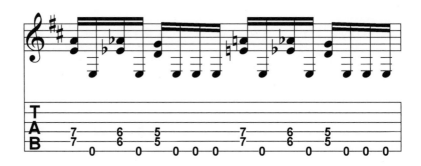

Scan to **HEAR** the C major chord, and
access the full library of scales and
chords on flametreemusic.com

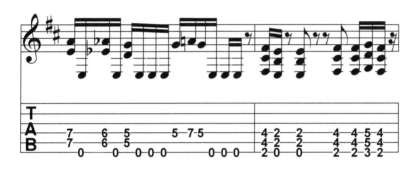

Scan to **HEAR** the C major chord, and access the full library of scales and chords on flametreemusic.com

START HERE

BASICS

BLUES

EARLY ROCK

PROG ROCK

HARD ROCK

SOFT ROCK

INDIE ROCK

Jimmy Page
(Led Zeppelin)

START HERE

BASICS

BLUES

EARLY ROCK

PROG ROCK

HARD ROCK

SOFT ROCK

INDIE ROCK

A5

Joe Perry
(Aerosmith)

START
HERE

BASICS

BLUES

EARLY
ROCK

PROG
ROCK

HARD
ROCK

SOFT
ROCK

INDIE
ROCK

♩ = 84

E5

C7

Scan to **HEAR** the C major chord, and
access the full library of scales and
chords on flametreemusic.com

START
HERE

BASICS

BLUES

EARLY
ROCK

PROG
ROCK

HARD
ROCK

SOFT
ROCK

INDIE
ROCK

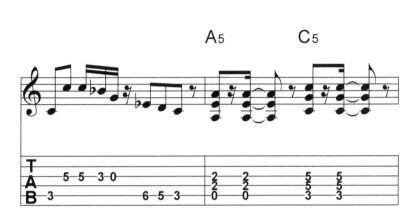

A5   C5

D5   E5

FREE ACCESS on iPhone & Android etc, using any free QR code app

Scan to **HEAR** the C major chord, and access the full library of scales and chords on flametreemusic.com

Randy Rhoads
(Ozzy Osbourne)

START
HERE

BASICS

BLUES

EARLY
ROCK

PROG
ROCK

HARD
ROCK

SOFT
ROCK

INDIE
ROCK

FREE ACCESS on iPhone & Android etc, using any free QR code app

Scan to **HEAR** the C major chord, and access the full library of scales and chords on flametreemusic.com

START
HERE

BASICS

BLUES

EARLY
ROCK

PROG
ROCK

HARD
ROCK

SOFT
ROCK

INDIE
ROCK

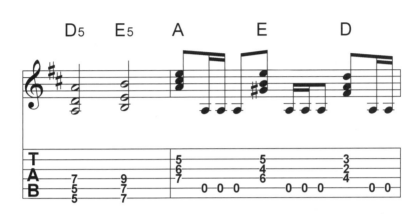

Scan to **HEAR** the C major chord, and
access the full library of scales and
chords on flametreemusic.com

Uli Jon Roth
(Scorpions)

START
HERE

BASICS

BLUES

EARLY
ROCK

PROG
ROCK

HARD
ROCK

SOFT
ROCK

INDIE
ROCK

♩ = 92

N.C.

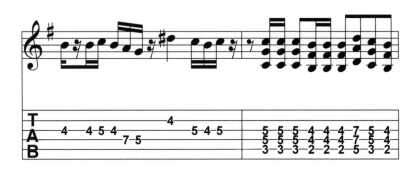

FREE ACCESS on iPhone & Android
etc, using any free QR code app

Scan to **HEAR** the C major chord, and
access the full library of scales and
chords on flametreemusic.com

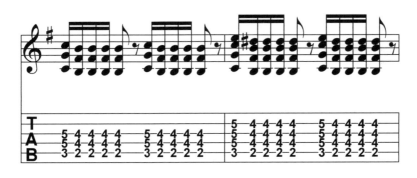

Scan to **HEAR** the C major chord, and access the full library of scales and chords on flametreemusic.com

Richie Sambora
(Bon Jovi)

♩ = 132

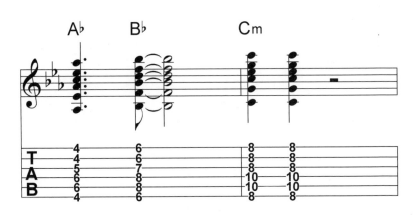

FREE ACCESS on iPhone & Android etc, using any free QR code app

Scan to **HEAR** the C major chord, and access the full library of scales and chords on flametreemusic.com

START HERE

BASICS

BLUES

EARLY ROCK

PROG ROCK

HARD ROCK

SOFT ROCK

INDIE ROCK

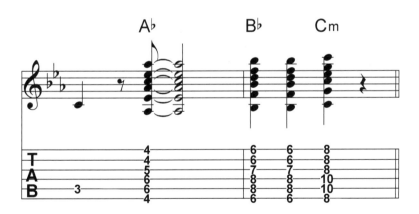

Joe Satriani

START
HERE

BASICS

BLUES

EARLY
ROCK

PROG
ROCK

HARD
ROCK

SOFT
ROCK

INDIE
ROCK

♩ = 140

B   G#m

E6   F#

FREE ACCESS on iPhone & Android
etc, using any free QR code app

Scan to **HEAR** the C major chord, and
access the full library of scales and
chords on flametreemusic.com

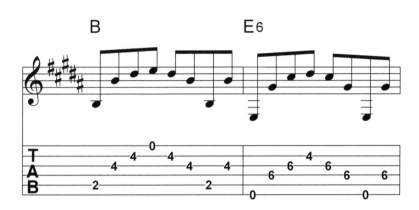

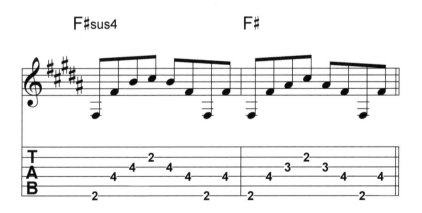

Scan to **HEAR** the C major chord, and access the full library of scales and chords on flametreemusic.com

Slash
(Guns N' Roses)

START HERE

BASICS

BLUES

EARLY ROCK

PROG ROCK

HARD ROCK

SOFT ROCK

INDIE ROCK

♩ = 164

A5

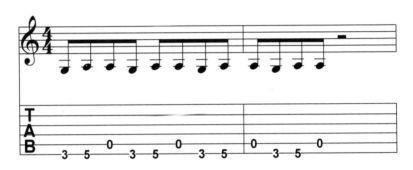

D5

FREE ACCESS on iPhone & Android etc, using any free QR code app

Scan to **HEAR** the C major chord, and access the full library of scales and chords on flametreemusic.com

A5

G5   **A5**   **G5**   **A5**

Scan to **HEAR** the C major chord, and access the full library of scales and chords on flametreemusic.com

Glenn Tipton
(Judas Priest)

START HERE

BASICS

BLUES

EARLY ROCK

PROG ROCK

HARD ROCK

SOFT ROCK

INDIE ROCK

FREE ACCESS on iPhone & Android
etc, using any free QR code app

Scan to HEAR the C major chord, and
access the full library of scales and
chords on flametreemusic.com

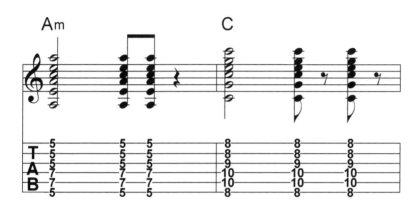

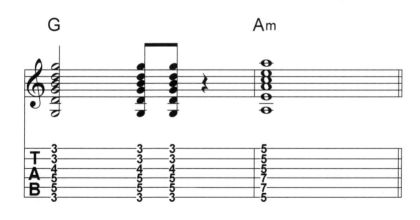

START HERE

BASICS

BLUES

EARLY ROCK

PROG ROCK

HARD ROCK

SOFT ROCK

INDIE ROCK

FREE ACCESS on iPhone & Android etc, using any free QR code app

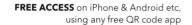

Scan to **HEAR** the C major chord, and access the full library of scales and chords on flametreemusic.com

Eddie Van Halen
(Van Halen)

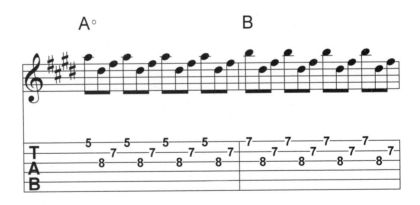

Scan to **HEAR** the C major chord, and
access the full library of scales and
chords on flametreemusic.com

START HERE

BASICS

BLUES

EARLY ROCK

PROG ROCK

HARD ROCK

SOFT ROCK

INDIE ROCK

START
HERE

BASICS

BLUES

EARLY
ROCK

PROG
ROCK

HARD
ROCK

SOFT
ROCK

INDIE
ROCK

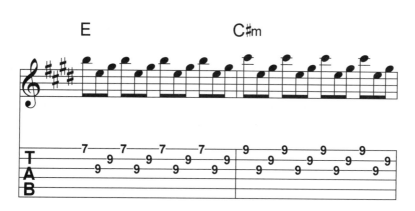

FREE ACCESS on iPhone & Android etc, using any free QR code app

Scan to **HEAR** the C major chord, and access the full library of scales and chords on flametreemusic.com

Angus & Malcolm Young
(AC/DC)

START
HERE

BASICS

BLUES

EARLY
ROCK

PROG
ROCK

HARD
ROCK

SOFT
ROCK

INDIE
ROCK

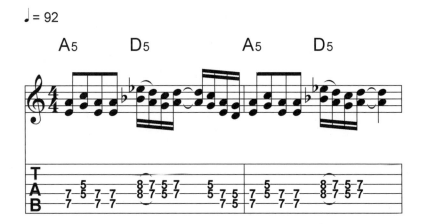

FREE ACCESS on iPhone & Android
etc, using any free QR code app

Scan to HEAR the C major chord, and
access the full library of scales and
chords on flametreemusic.com

D5   A5 G5 A5

Scan to **HEAR** the C major chord, and access the full library of scales and chords on flametreemusic.com

START HERE

BASICS

BLUES

EARLY ROCK

PROG ROCK

HARD ROCK

SOFT ROCK

INDIE ROCK

START
HERE

BASICS

BLUES

EARLY
ROCK

PROG
ROCK

HARD
ROCK

SOFT
ROCK

INDIE
ROCK

Funk, Soft Rock & Pop

Rock has its softer, smoother, more melodic sides, which swing dangerously close to pop.

The roots of this reach back to Hank Marvin's smooth, elegant lines in *The Shadows* of the early Sixties, but more than a decade later this flowered into a succession of cracking guitarists who wore their riffs cloaked in smart, listener-friendly melodies. From the electro-pulse of *U2*'s The Edge to the tasteful, almost folksy licks of Mark Knopfler, rock's rebelliousness was being subsumed into the mainstream. There were some wilder outposts: Andy Summer's Jazzy lines in *The Police*, for example, were encased in some of the best pop tunes of the late twentieth century.

As with all the riffs in this book, it may help to watch some clips of the guitarists playing their own music: look out, for example, for their preferred picking patterns, where on the guitar neck they are playing, and their general technique.

This section includes riffs in the style of the following artists:

- The Edge (U2)
- Peter Frampton
- George Harrison (The Beatles)
- Davey Johnstone (Elton John)
- Mark Knopfler (Dire Straits)
- Lenny Kravitz
- Hank Marvin (The Shadows)
- Roger McGuinn (The Byrds)
- Mick Ronson (David Bowie)
- Andy Summers (The Police)

FREE ACCESS on iPhone & Android etc, using any free QR code app

Scan to **HEAR** the C major chord, and access the full library of scales and chords on flametreemusic.com

START
HERE

BASICS

BLUES

EARLY
ROCK

PROG
ROCK

HARD
ROCK

SOFT
ROCK

INDIE
ROCK

FREE ACCESS on iPhone & Android etc,
using any free QR code app

Scan to **HEAR** the C major chord, and
access the full library of scales and
chords on flametreemusic.com

The Edge
(U2)

START
HERE

BASICS

BLUES

EARLY
ROCK

PROG
ROCK

HARD
ROCK

SOFT
ROCK

INDIE
ROCK

♩ = 140

FREE ACCESS on iPhone & Android
etc, using any free QR code app

Scan to **HEAR** the C major chord, and
access the full library of scales and
chords on flametreemusic.com

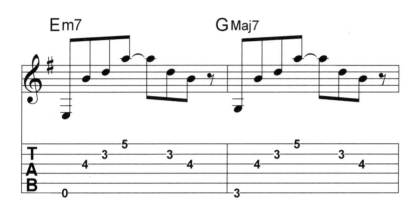

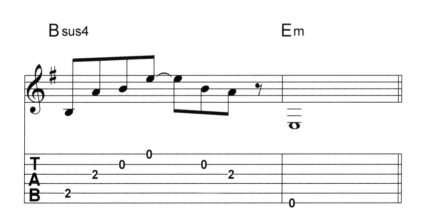

START
HERE

BASICS

BLUES

EARLY
ROCK

PROG
ROCK

HARD
ROCK

SOFT
ROCK

INDIE
ROCK

FREE ACCESS on iPhone & Android etc,
using any free QR code app

Scan to **HEAR** the C major chord, and
access the full library of scales and
chords on flametreemusic.com

Peter Frampton

START
HERE

BASICS

BLUES

EARLY
ROCK

PROG
ROCK

HARD
ROCK

SOFT
ROCK

INDIE
ROCK

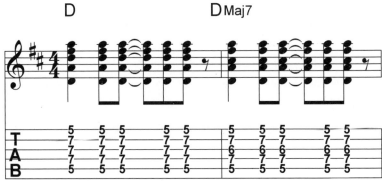

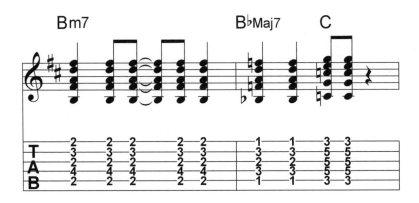

FREE ACCESS on iPhone & Android
etc, using any free QR code app

Scan to **HEAR** the C major chord, and
access the full library of scales and
chords on flametreemusic.com

START
HERE

BASICS

BLUES

EARLY
ROCK

PROG
ROCK

HARD
ROCK

SOFT
ROCK

INDIE
ROCK

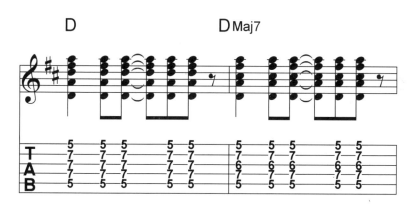

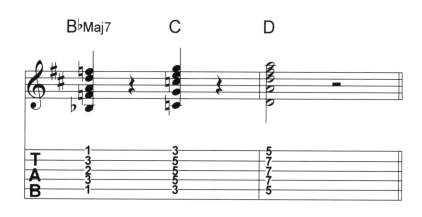

FREE ACCESS on iPhone & Android etc,
using any free QR code app

Scan to HEAR the C major chord, and
access the full library of scales and
chords on flametreemusic.com

George Harrison
(The Beatles)

START
HERE

BASICS

BLUES

EARLY
ROCK

PROG
ROCK

HARD
ROCK

SOFT
ROCK

INDIE
ROCK

♩ = 80

FREE ACCESS on iPhone & Android
etc, using any free QR code app

Scan to **HEAR** the C major chord, and
access the full library of scales and
chords on flametreemusic.com

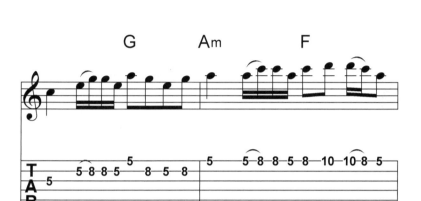

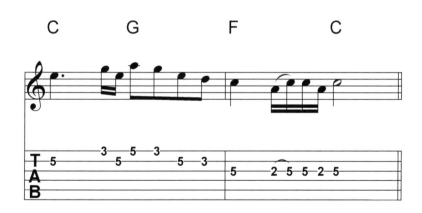

START
HERE

BASICS

BLUES

EARLY
ROCK

PROG
ROCK

HARD
ROCK

SOFT
ROCK

INDIE
ROCK

FREE ACCESS on iPhone & Android etc,
using any free QR code app

Scan to **HEAR** the C major chord, and
access the full library of scales and
chords on flametreemusic.com

Davey Johnstone
(Elton John)

START
HERE

BASICS

BLUES

EARLY
ROCK

PROG
ROCK

HARD
ROCK

SOFT
ROCK

INDIE
ROCK

♩ = 84

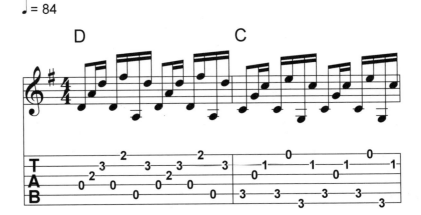

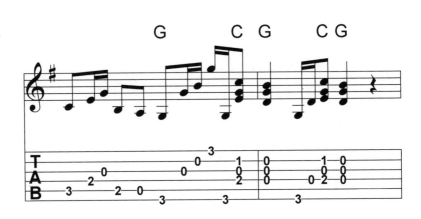

FREE ACCESS on iPhone & Android
etc, using any free QR code app

Scan to **HEAR** the C major chord, and
access the full library of scales and
chords on flametreemusic.com

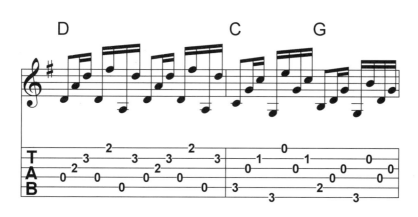

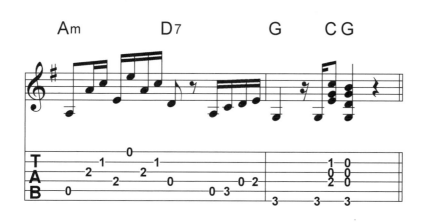

START
HERE

BASICS

BLUES

EARLY
ROCK

PROG
ROCK

HARD
ROCK

SOFT
ROCK

INDIE
ROCK

FREE ACCESS on iPhone & Android etc, using any free QR code app

Scan to **HEAR** the C major chord, and access the full library of scales and chords on flametreemusic.com

Mark Knopfler
(Dire Straits)

START
HERE

BASICS

BLUES

EARLY
ROCK

PROG
ROCK

HARD
ROCK

SOFT
ROCK

INDIE
ROCK

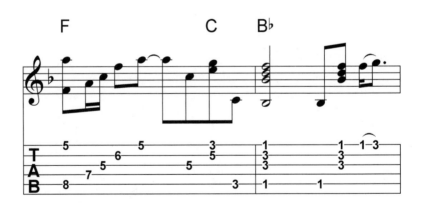

Scan to **HEAR** the C major chord, and
access the full library of scales and
chords on flametreemusic.com

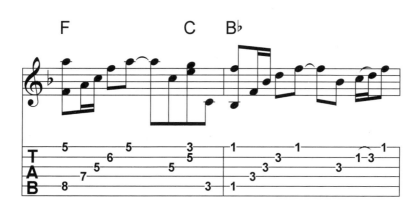

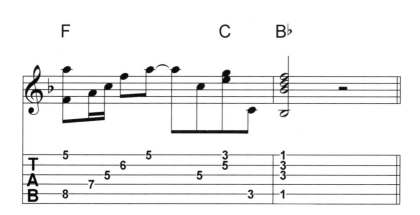

FREE ACCESS on iPhone & Android etc, using any free QR code app

Scan to **HEAR** the C major chord, and access the full library of scales and chords on flametreemusic.com

START HERE

BASICS

BLUES

EARLY ROCK

PROG ROCK

HARD ROCK

SOFT ROCK

INDIE ROCK

Lenny Kravitz

Scan to **HEAR** the C major chord, and
access the full library of scales and
chords on flametreemusic.com

FREE ACCESS on iPhone & Android etc,
using any free QR code app

Scan to **HEAR** the C major chord, and
access the full library of scales and
chords on flametreemusic.com

Hank Marvin
(The Shadows)

START
HERE

BASICS

BLUES

EARLY
ROCK

PROG
ROCK

HARD
ROCK

SOFT
ROCK

INDIE
ROCK

B♭   E

Am

Scan to **HEAR** the C major chord, and access the full library of scales and chords on flametreemusic.com

START HERE

BASICS

BLUES

EARLY ROCK

PROG ROCK

HARD ROCK

SOFT ROCK

INDIE ROCK

Roger McGuinn
(The Byrds)

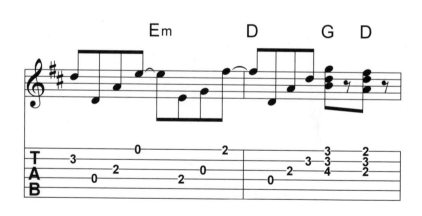

FREE ACCESS on iPhone & Android etc, using any free QR code app

Scan to **HEAR** the C major chord, and access the full library of scales and chords on flametreemusic.com

START HERE

BASICS

BLUES

EARLY ROCK

PROG ROCK

HARD ROCK

SOFT ROCK

INDIE ROCK

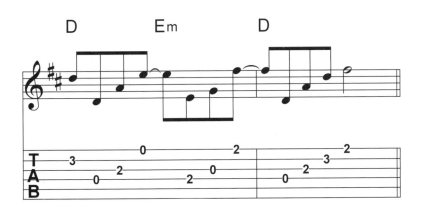

Scan to **HEAR** the C major chord, and
access the full library of scales and
chords on flametreemusic.com

Mick Ronson
(David Bowie)

START HERE

BASICS

BLUES

EARLY ROCK

PROG ROCK

HARD ROCK

SOFT ROCK

INDIE ROCK

♩ = 76

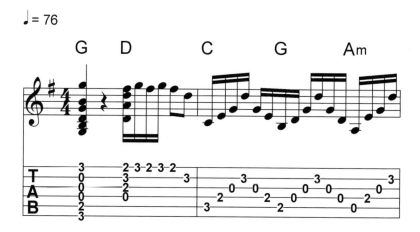

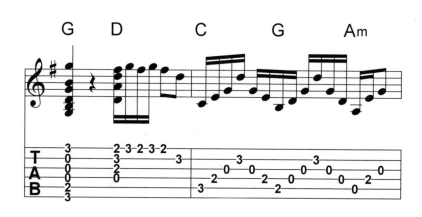

FREE ACCESS on iPhone & Android etc, using any free QR code app

Scan to **HEAR** the C major chord, and access the full library of scales and chords on flametreemusic.com

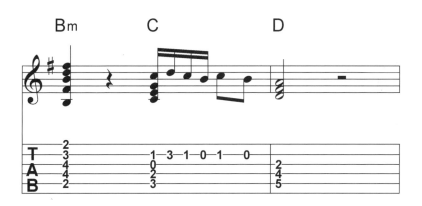

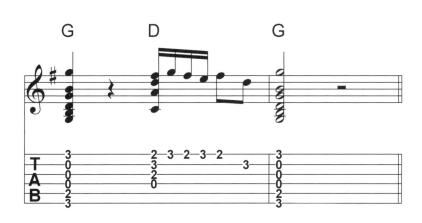

FREE ACCESS on iPhone & Android etc, using any free QR code app

Scan to **HEAR** the C major chord, and access the full library of scales and chords on flametreemusic.com

START HERE

BASICS

BLUES

EARLY ROCK

PROG ROCK

HARD ROCK

SOFT ROCK

INDIE ROCK

Andy Summers
(The Police)

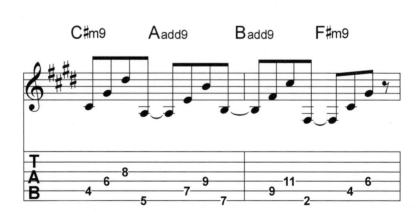

FREE ACCESS on iPhone & Android
etc, using any free QR code app

Scan to **HEAR** the C major chord, and
access the full library of scales and
chords on flametreemusic.com

146

START
HERE

BASICS

BLUES

EARLY
ROCK

PROG
ROCK

HARD
ROCK

SOFT
ROCK

INDIE
ROCK

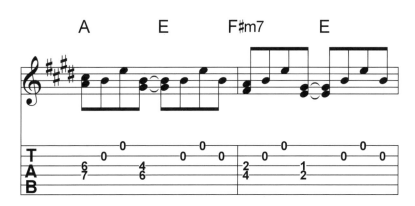

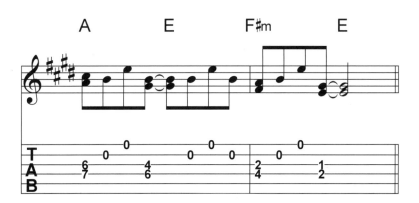

Punk, Alternative & Indie Rock

One of the most powerful aspects of rock music is its ability to create and recreate a constant rebellion against itself.

As *The Who* sang in 'Won't Get Fooled Again', 'Meet the new boss, Same as the old boss'. In rock, as in life, the rebels take over the establishment and spawn a new generation of rebels. The punk explosion of the Seventies opened the door to successive generations of simple, direct challenges to the royalties of rock. For some, the rebellion is expressed through a rejection of lead-guitar breaks and melodies; for others it's the blistering capture of retro rock, like Jack White in *The White Stripes*, or Graham Coxon's gobby rhythm chops on his post-*Blur* solo albums.

This section includes riffs in the style of the following artists:

- Matt Bellamy (Muse)
- James Dean Bradfield (Manic Street Preachers)
- Peter Buck (R.E.M.)
- Bernard Butler (Suede)
- Kurt Cobain (Nirvana)
- Graham Coxon (Blur)
- John Frusciante (Red Hot Chili Peppers)
- Adam Jones (Tool)
- Johnny Marr (The Smiths)
- Tom Morello (Rage Against the Machine)
- Tom Verlaine (Television)
- Jack White (The White Stripes)
- Neil Young

START HERE

BASICS

BLUES

EARLY ROCK

PROG ROCK

HARD ROCK

SOFT ROCK

INDIE ROCK

FREE ACCESS on iPhone & Android etc, using any free QR code app

Scan to **HEAR** the C major chord, and access the full library of scales and chords on flametreemusic.com

START HERE

BASICS

BLUES

EARLY ROCK

PROG ROCK

HARD ROCK

SOFT ROCK

INDIE ROCK

FREE ACCESS on iPhone & Android etc, using any free QR code app

Scan to **HEAR** the C major chord, and access the full library of scales and chords on flametreemusic.com

Matt Bellamy
(Muse)

START
HERE

BASICS

BLUES

EARLY
ROCK

PROG
ROCK

HARD
ROCK

SOFT
ROCK

INDIE
ROCK

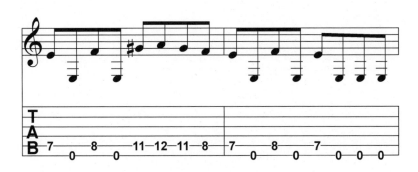

Scan to **HEAR** the C major chord, and
access the full library of scales and
chords on flametreemusic.com

START
HERE

BASICS

BLUES

EARLY
ROCK

PROG
ROCK

HARD
ROCK

SOFT
ROCK

INDIE
ROCK

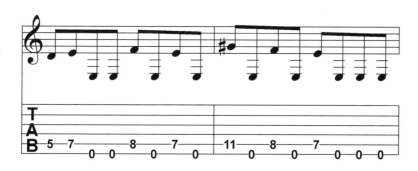

FREE ACCESS on iPhone & Android
etc, using any free QR code app

Scan to **HEAR** the C major chord, and
access the full library of scales and
chords on flametreemusic.com

James Dean Bradfield
(Manic Street Preachers)

START
HERE

BASICS

BLUES

EARLY
ROCK

PROG
ROCK

HARD
ROCK

SOFT
ROCK

INDIE
ROCK

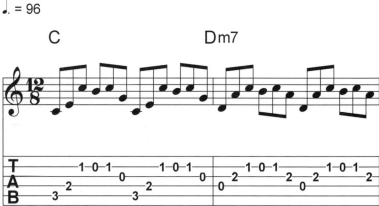

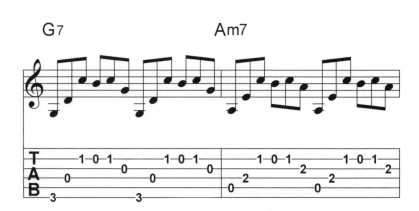

Scan to **HEAR** the C major chord, and access the full library of scales and chords on flametreemusic.com

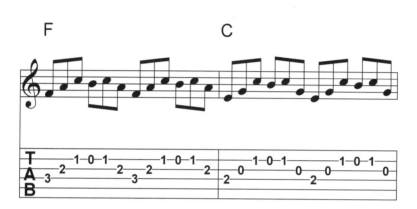

Scan to **HEAR** the C major chord, and access the full library of scales and chords on flametreemusic.com

START HERE

BASICS

BLUES

EARLY ROCK

PROG ROCK

HARD ROCK

SOFT ROCK

INDIE ROCK

Peter Buck
(R.E.M.)

START HERE

BASICS

BLUES

EARLY ROCK

PROG ROCK

HARD ROCK

SOFT ROCK

INDIE ROCK

♩. = 96

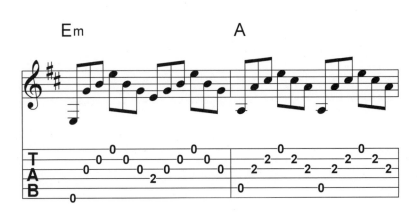

FREE ACCESS on iPhone & Android
etc, using any free QR code app

Scan to HEAR the C major chord, and
access the full library of scales and
chords on flametreemusic.com

START
HERE

BASICS

BLUES

EARLY
ROCK

PROG
ROCK

HARD
ROCK

SOFT
ROCK

INDIE
ROCK

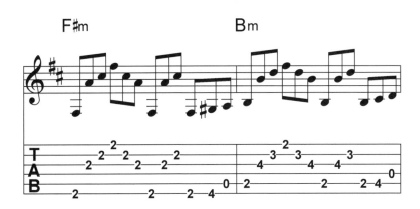

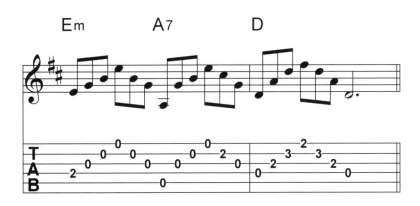

FREE ACCESS on iPhone & Android
etc, using any free QR code app

Scan to **HEAR** the C major chord, and
access the full library of scales and
chords on flametreemusic.com

155

Bernard Butler
(Suede)

START
HERE

BASICS

BLUES

EARLY
ROCK

PROG
ROCK

HARD
ROCK

SOFT
ROCK

**INDIE
ROCK**

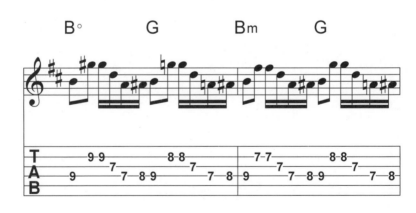

FREE ACCESS on iPhone & Android
etc, using any free QR code app

Scan to **HEAR** the C major chord, and
access the full library of scales and
chords on flametreemusic.com

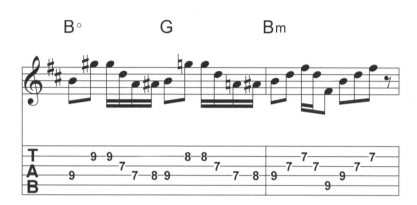

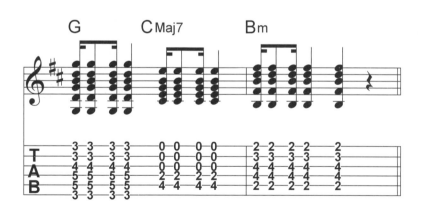

START HERE

BASICS

BLUES

EARLY ROCK

PROG ROCK

HARD ROCK

SOFT ROCK

INDIE ROCK

FREE ACCESS on iPhone & Android etc, using any free QR code app

Scan to **HEAR** the C major chord, and access the full library of scales and chords on flametreemusic.com

Kurt Cobain
(Nirvana)

START HERE

BASICS

BLUES

EARLY ROCK

PROG ROCK

HARD ROCK

SOFT ROCK

INDIE ROCK

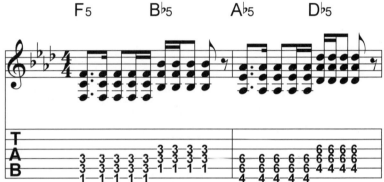

FREE ACCESS on iPhone & Android
etc, using any free QR code app

Scan to **HEAR** the C major chord, and
access the full library of scales and
chords on flametreemusic.com

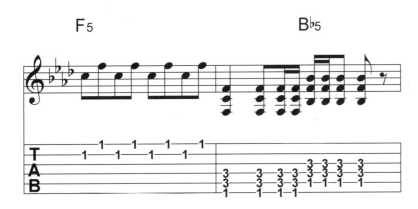

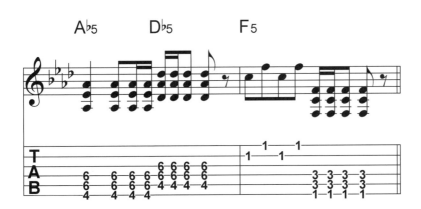

Scan to **HEAR** the C major chord, and access the full library of scales and chords on flametreemusic.com

START HERE

BASICS

BLUES

EARLY ROCK

PROG ROCK

HARD ROCK

SOFT ROCK

INDIE ROCK

Graham Coxon
(Blur)

START
HERE

BASICS

BLUES

EARLY
ROCK

PROG
ROCK

HARD
ROCK

SOFT
ROCK

INDIE
ROCK

START HERE

BASICS

BLUES

EARLY ROCK

PROG ROCK

HARD ROCK

SOFT ROCK

INDIE ROCK

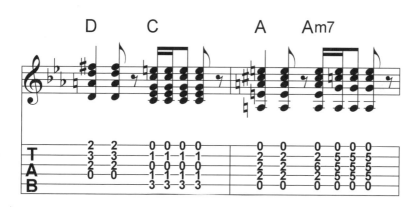

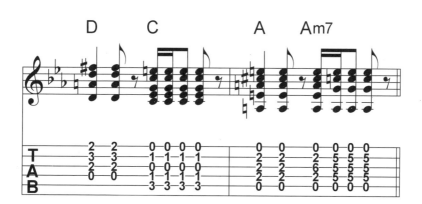

FREE ACCESS on iPhone & Android etc, using any free QR code app

Scan to **HEAR** the C major chord, and access the full library of scales and chords on flametreemusic.com

John Frusciante
(Red Hot Chili Peppers)

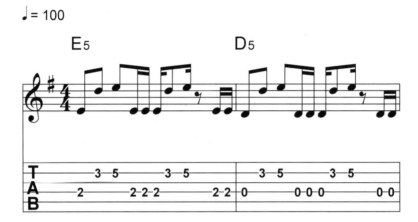

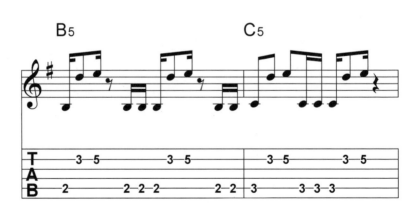

Scan to **HEAR** the C major chord, and
access the full library of scales and
chords on flametreemusic.com

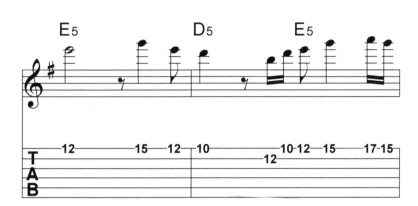

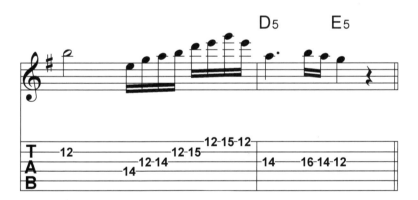

FREE ACCESS on iPhone & Android
etc, using any free QR code app

Scan to **HEAR** the C major chord, and
access the full library of scales and
chords on flametreemusic.com

START
HERE

BASICS

BLUES

EARLY
ROCK

PROG
ROCK

HARD
ROCK

SOFT
ROCK

INDIE
ROCK

Adam Jones
(Tool)

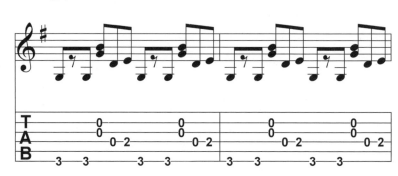

Scan to **HEAR** the C major chord, and
access the full library of scales and
chords on flametreemusic.com

FREE ACCESS on iPhone & Android etc, using any free QR code app

Scan to **HEAR** the C major chord, and access the full library of scales and chords on flametreemusic.com

START HERE

BASICS

BLUES

EARLY ROCK

PROG ROCK

HARD ROCK

SOFT ROCK

INDIE ROCK

Johnny Marr
(The Smiths)

START
HERE

BASICS

BLUES

EARLY
ROCK

PROG
ROCK

HARD
ROCK

SOFT
ROCK

INDIE
ROCK

Scan to **HEAR** the C major chord, and
access the full library of scales and
chords on flametreemusic.com

START
HERE

BASICS

BLUES

EARLY
ROCK

PROG
ROCK

HARD
ROCK

SOFT
ROCK

**INDIE
ROCK**

FREE ACCESS on iPhone & Android
etc, using any free QR code app

Scan to **HEAR** the C major chord, and
access the full library of scales and
chords on flametreemusic.com

Tom Morello
(Rage Against the Machine)

START
HERE

BASICS

BLUES

EARLY
ROCK

PROG
ROCK

HARD
ROCK

SOFT
ROCK

INDIE
ROCK

FREE ACCESS on iPhone & Android
etc, using any free QR code app

Scan to **HEAR** the C major chord, and
access the full library of scales and
chords on flametreemusic.com

START
HERE

BASICS

BLUES

EARLY
ROCK

PROG
ROCK

HARD
ROCK

SOFT
ROCK

INDIE
ROCK

FREE ACCESS on iPhone & Android
etc, using any free QR code app

Scan to **HEAR** the C major chord, and
access the full library of scales and
chords on flametreemusic.com

Tom Verlaine
(Television)

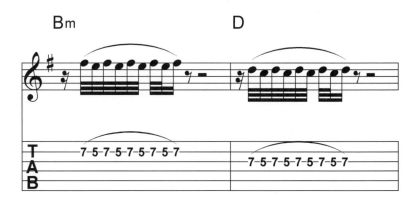

Scan to **HEAR** the C major chord, and
access the full library of scales and
chords on flametreemusic.com

START
HERE

BASICS

BLUES

EARLY
ROCK

PROG
ROCK

HARD
ROCK

SOFT
ROCK

INDIE
ROCK

FREE ACCESS on iPhone & Android
etc, using any free QR code app

Scan to **HEAR** the C major chord, and
access the full library of scales and
chords on flametreemusic.com

Jack White
(The White Stripes)

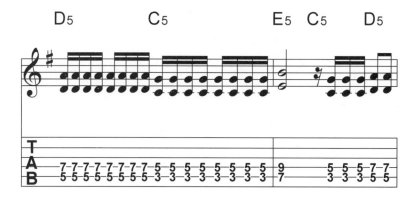

FREE ACCESS on iPhone & Android
etc, using any free QR code app

Scan to **HEAR** the C major chord, and
access the full library of scales and
chords on flametreemusic.com

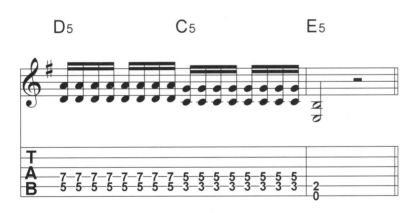

Scan to **HEAR** the C major chord, and access the full library of scales and chords on flametreemusic.com

Neil Young

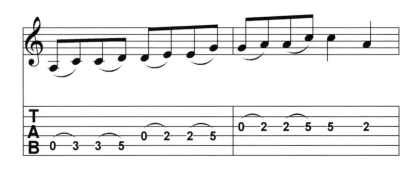

START HERE

BASICS

BLUES

EARLY ROCK

PROG ROCK

HARD ROCK

SOFT ROCK

INDIE ROCK

FREE ACCESS on iPhone & Android etc, using any free QR code app

Scan to **HEAR** the C major chord, and access the full library of scales and chords on flametreemusic.com

Scan to **HEAR** the C major chord, and access the full library of scales and chords on flametreemusic.com

START HERE

BASICS

BLUES

EARLY ROCK

PROG ROCK

HARD ROCK

SOFT ROCK

INDIE ROCK

flametreemusic.com

The Flame Tree Music website complements our range of print books and offers easy access to chords and scales online, and on the move, through tablets, smartphones, and desktop computers.

1. The site offers access to chord diagrams and finger positions for both the guitar and the piano/keyboard, presenting a wide range of sound options to help develop good listening technique, and to assist you in identifying the chord and each note within it.

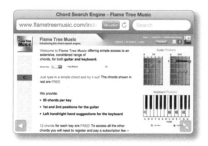

2. The site offers 12 **free** chords, those most commonly used in bands and songwriting.

3. A subscription is available if you'd like the full range of chords, **50** for **each key**.

4. Guitar chords are shown with **first** and **second positions on the fretboard**.

5. For the keyboard, you can **see** and **hear** each note in **left-** and **right-hand positions**.

6. Choose the key, then the chord name from the drop down menu. Note that the **red chords** are available **free**. Those in blue can be accessed with a subscription.

7. Once you've selected the chord, press **GO** and the details of the chord will be shown, with chord spellings, keyboard and guitar fingerings.

8. Sounds are provided in four easy-to-understand configurations.

9. flametreemusic.com also gives you access to **20 scales for each key**.